# BIBLE CHARACTERS AND DOCTRINES

**Bathsheba to Rehoboam**

E. M. BLAIKLOCK, M.A., D.Litt.

**Man and Sin**

A. SKEVINGTON WOOD, B.A., Ph.D.,
F.R. Hist. S.

WILLIAM B. EERDMANS PUBLISHING COMPANY
GRAND RAPIDS, MICHIGAN

© 1972 Scripture Union
First published 1972
First USA edition published January 1973

SCRIPTURE UNION IN NORTH AMERICA

U. S. A.:  38 Garrett Road, Upper Darby,
          Pennsylvania 19082
Canada:   5 Rowanwood Avenue, Toronto 5,
          Ontario

Printed in the United States of America.

# Introduction

Each volume of Bible Characters and Doctrines is divided into the right number of sections to make daily use possible, though dates are not attached to the sections because of the books' continuing use as a complete set of character studies and doctrinal expositions. The study for each day is clearly numbered and the Bible passage to be read is placed alongside it.

Sections presenting the characters and doctrines alternate throughout each book, providing balance and variety in the selected subjects. At the end of each section there is a selection of questions and themes for further study related to the material covered in the preceding readings.

Each volume will provide material for one quarter's use, with between 91 and 96 sections. Where it is suggested that two sections should be read together in order to fit the three-month period, they are marked with an asterisk.

The scheme will be completed in four years. Professor E. M. Blaiklock, who writes all the character studies, will work progressively through the Old and New Testament records. Writers of the doctrinal sections contribute to a pattern of studies drawn up by the Rev. Geoffrey Grogan, Principal of the Bible Training Institute, Glasgow, in his capacity as Co-ordinating Editor. A chart overleaf indicates how the doctrinal sections are planned.

In this series biblical quotations are normally taken from the RSV unless otherwise identified. Occasionally Professor Blaiklock provides his own translation of the biblical text.

## DOCTRINAL STUDY SCHEME

|  | Year 1 | Year 2 | Year 3 | Year 4 |
|---|---|---|---|---|
| First Quarter | The God who Speaks | Man and Sin | The Work of Christ | The Kingdom and the Church |
| Second Quarter | God in His World | Law and Grace | Righteousness in Christ | The Mission of the Church |
| Third Quarter | The Character of God | The Life of Christ | Life in Christ | The Church's Ministry and Ordinances |
| Fourth Quarter | The Holy Trinity | The Person of Christ | The Holy Spirit | The Last Things |

# DOCTRINAL STUDIES
## MAN AND SIN

Study

## A Guilty Rebel: Convicted by the Prophets

## A Guilty Rebel: Recognized and Rebuked in the New Testament

## A Helpless Slave

# CHARACTER STUDIES
## BATHSHEBA TO REHOBOAM

# MAN AND SIN

## INTRODUCTION

Ours is the era of man. He is now regarded as having come of age. As one who has succeeded in decoding the universe, he holds the cosmic stage. Belief in God has waned: belief in man is strong. As a result, it is a curious fact that more interest is likely to be displayed today in what Christianity has to say about man than about God. Even though the theological presuppositions of the Christian faith are largely rejected, there is a renewed readiness to consider the biblical estimate of man, along with other views, as a contribution to an overall assessment of his nature and potential.

From the standpoint of the Bible, however, any attempt to arrive at a verdict on man which sets aside his relationship to God is an obvious non-starter. The dominant theme of Scripture is centrally not of man but of God. Christian doctrine is concerned with theology rather than anthropology. It is axiomatic in the Word that man has no significance apart from God. He can only be construed in terms of his dependence on the creator. As Emil Brunner insisted, 'his relation to God is not something which is added to his human nature; it is the core and the ground of his *humanitas*.'

This is why the bare question, 'What is man?' is never raised in Scripture. It is evidently assumed that the answer would lack importance. Man apart from God is no more than a dream, a mist, or the ephemeral grass-growth of a Palestinian field (Psa. **90**. 5f.; Jas. **4**.14). The psalmist enquires not about man in himself but about man in relation to God: 'What is man that thou art mindful of him?' (Psa. **8**.4). It is only because God is interested in him that man possesses any real significance at all (cf. Job **7**.11 ff.). Indeed, it is only as he is made aware of God that he realizes himself fully as a person. Self-consciousness was originally a product of God-consciousness.

The Bible presents man in a dual aspect, whilst treating him essentially as a unity. On the one hand he is a finite creature who is a homogeneous part of the universe. He was made from the dust (Gen. **2**.7) and belongs to the animal

9

kingdom. Whatever transcendent features he may display, this continuity with nature is an inescapable fact. To read Desmond Morris's *The Naked Ape* and *The Human Zoo* can be a salutary experience, for although the biological view of man does not tell the whole story, we are at least cut down to size and reminded of our essential creatureliness.

But the Bible does not leave it at that, as Morris appears to do. Man is much more than an animal. He is unique in creation, since he bears the image of God. He is a person who feels, thinks and wills. He can consciously commune with his Maker. His final destiny is to enjoy such fellowship for ever. Even here on earth he is meant to live as a son of God.

His own rebellion, however, has intervened to jeopardize his relation to God and prevent him from realizing his potential. Because he has wilfully snatched at the authority which belongs only to God, he now finds himself frustrated and unfulfilled. Despite his growing mastery over nature, he is the victim of a death wish which could ultimately lead to his own destruction. This elemental resistance to the loving will of God the Bible describes as sin. Whilst man remains in the grip of such self-imposed slavery, he can never achieve integration and fulfilment. His goal can be reached only in Christ, the second Adam, in whom God has expressed the new humanity which is His ideal for every man. It remains true that, as Stephen Neill has put it, a 'man is only a man when he is like God and lives in fellowship with Him.'

This, in brief, is the biblical view of man and sin. In the studies which follow, the pattern will be traced in greater detail through the exposition of crucial passages. These are not directly linked with each other, as the reader will discover, but together they reflect some of the major emphases to be considered in the articulation of these highly relevant doctrines.

Amongst the standard works of the past on the biblical teaching about man are J. Laidlaw, *The Bible Doctrine of Man* (1895), H. W. Robinson, *The Christian Doctrine of Man* (1911), and J. G. Machen, *The Christian View of Man* (1937). More recent studies include E. Brunner, *Man in Revolt* (ET 1939), R. Niebuhr, *The Nature and Destiny of Man* (2 vols. 1941-3), D. Cairns, *The Image of God in Man* (1953), and E. Sauer, *The King of the Earth* (1962). On sin, see C. R. Smith, *The Bible Doctrine of Sin* (1953), and F. Greeves, *The Meaning of Sin* (1956).

# MAN AND SIN

## God's Creature

### 1 : In the Image of God

#### Genesis 1.26–2.9, 15–25

The biblical and scientific accounts of man's origins agree in regarding him as the crown of creation. In Genesis both his affinity with the natural world and his superiority to it are equally stressed. He was fashioned from the dust and yet created in God's own image (2.7; 1.27). This combination supplies the key to man's complex nature. Scripture is sufficiently realistic to do justice to each of the elements involved.

The verb to create (bārā') stands for 'that divine creativity which is absolutely without analogy' (G. von Rad). It is included three times in one verse (1.27) as if to emphasize the uniqueness of man. The creative action is introduced, moreover, with a distinct divine resolution (1.26), indicating that God was here implicated more fully and closely than in His former works.

The specific feature in man which marks him off from the rest of creation is described as the image of God. 'Likeness' in 1.26 is simply an explanatory qualification. These complementary terms strongly assert that man in some way reflects his Creator. He shares the personhood of God. He is a self-conscious, rational, responsible being. Here lies his highest dignity (Gen. 9.6). In view of this fact, it is not surprising that there is widespread dissatisfaction among young people with the materialism (both theoretical and practical) of the present age. God made man with a spiritual dimension and this seeks fulfilment. The devil is not slow in supplying 'spiritual' alternatives to the gospel!

It is as one created in God's image that man can enter into dialogue with Him. This is what shows man to be a son of God, just as Seth was said to be after the image of Adam (Gen. 5.3). But the image cannot be maintained independ-

11

ently of the One whom it expresses. Hence the significance of 'breath' in **2**.7. To be sure the same divine spirit conveys life to all animate creatures. Yet its function is to maintain what God has bestowed, and in the case of man this endowment is God's image.

As one who thus partakes of the divine nature (2 Pet. **1**.4) man reproduces himself in procreation and exercises dominion over the earth and its creatures (Gen. **1**.28). Like his Maker, man is both father and lord. Such was God's intention for him, and in such unsullied innocence and undisputed sovereignty he would presumably have continued had sin not intervened.

As we have seen, Gen. **2**.7 reminds us that the physical differentiation between man and the animals is a matter of quality and not of substance. 'Breath of life' and 'living being' are not expressions confined to the human species (cf. Gen. **1**.21, 24, 30; **2**.19). Only in the case of man, however, is there a direct transfer of *rûah* by a special divine insufflation, and only in one like himself does he find an appropriate companion (**2**.18).

*A thought : I ought never to 'put on a pedestal' nor to underrate a creature of God, made in His image.*


## 2 : Man's Littleness and Greatness

### Psalm 8

The psalmist sees man first in relation to God and then in relation to the world of created things. When set in the sight of God he seems small indeed, but as over against the animal kingdom he is impressively great. Psa. **8** has been described as 'a poetic replica of the creation narrative of Genesis **1** so far as it refers to man' (J. Laidlaw). It is a meditation on the creation of man as envisaged retrospectively through the fall.

Man's comparative insignificance is apparent not only as he is measured against the majesty of God (1), but also as he is placed in the context of the universe (3). He is no more than a speck of dust in the immensity of space. But this is to assess him purely in dimensional terms. Such a verdict overlooks the status God has bestowed on man. God has crowned him with glory and honour (5). Man, not nature, is the central theme of the Psalm. His God-given dignity is the real marvel of the universe.

'Wonders are many, and none is more wonderful than man,' wrote Sophocles in *Antigone*. But whereas Greek thought considered man's value to be inherent, the biblical revelation recognizes that it is solely of grace. Man's assets are what God has made over to him. That is why no realistic account of man can ignore his relationship to God. An age which denies God will inevitably fail to understand man. In Communism the interests of the individual are completely subordinate to those of the group. Man has no spiritual dimension. Religion is 'the opium of the people'. In some psychological theories man is little more than a very complex machine.

The true stature of man is measured by what God has made him. He falls only a little short of the angels (5, AV [as in the Septuagint and Vulgate], cf. Heb. 2.7f). In a strictly monotheistic context *Elóhîm* (the Hebrew word in v. 5) would appear to mean either God Himself (RSV, RV) or 'the inhabitants of heaven' (W. Eichrodt). The reference is to the image of God in man.

Man's dominion over the rest of creation is not seized by revolt, but received from God as a sacred trust (6). It is in stewardship that he controls the natural world (7 f.). In himself he is weak and insignificant. Under God alone can he claim to be the king of the earth. Recent interest in ecology, in conservation and pollution, testifies unconsciously to our responsibility to exercise this stewardship aright.

*Is my attitude towards the material things which are God's creation responsible and Christian?*

# 3 : The Miracle of Birth

## Psalm 139

The psalm is a paean of praise to God. It extols His omniscience (1–6), omnipresence (7–12), and omnipotence (13–18). Man is seen only in his dependence on his Creator. He is completely known to God. He has been subjected to the most searching scrutiny (3). Nothing is hidden from God. Nor can man hide himself. Even though he tries to escape, he cannot. The psalmist considers the various routes by which he might do so but decides that they are uniformly inadequate for the purpose.

He is led to dwell on the unlimited power of God. Psa. 8 illustrates the divine omnipotence by pointing to the creation of the universe (cf. also Psa. 104). Psa. 139 does so in terms of man's own origin. All that we now know about the process of human reproduction from conception to birth only serves to increase our wonder at the miracle. It is God who creates the inmost self, the essential personality, so as to claim possession of it (13). It is He who is responsible for the development of the embryo in the womb. Contemplation of the mystery can only call forth praise and gratitude (14). The bone structure of the human frame and the intricate interlacing of nerves, veins and muscles are all observed and indeed superintended by God. 'In the depths of the earth' (15) is used figuratively to describe 'the limbo of the womb' (JB). Elsewhere it refers to Sheol, the place of departed spirits (Psa. 63.9; 86.13). Here the womb is thought of as a dark underworld. We are not therefore to imagine some divine laboratory in the bowels of the earth.

'Unformed' (16) is literally 'rolled together' like a ball, and thus aptly applied to the foetus. Either all the days of the Psalmist's life are said to be entered in God's records, even before he was born (RSV, JB) or (more probably in the context of v. 16) all his limbs were similarly catalogued, and as they were fashioned 'not one of them was late in growing' (NEB). As he considers the incredible mystery of man's procreation, the Psalmist breaks out into renewed astonishment at the profundity and inexhaustibility of the divine wisdom (cf. Rom. 11.33). After announcing his hatred of the wicked who range themselves against such a gracious God (19–22), he returns to the theme of examination with which he began (23 f., cf. v. 1). Man's real well-being—my real well-being—consists in 'shunning every evil way, and walking in the good' (Charles Wesley).

# 4 : The Sanctity of Marriage

## Matthew 19.1–12

According to T. H. Robinson, 'this is the highest word ever uttered on marriage.' Our Lord's appeal under pressure from the Pharisees was not to the tradition of the elders but to Scripture. He referred His critics to their own final authority and cited Gen. **1**.27 and **2**.24 (4 f.).

The dispute focused on the interpretation of Deut. **24**.1, with its sanctioning of divorce. There could be no question that according to the Jewish law divorce was allowed on certain grounds. But what are those grounds? What is meant by the qualification about a wife falling out of favour because of something shameful? The stricter school of Shammai took this to mean adultery. The more liberal followers of Hillel broadened it to include anything which displeased the husband—even to burning his food when cooking it.

If the Pharisees hoped to trap Jesus into taking sides on this issue they were disappointed. He cut right through the web of rabbinical casuistry to reach the heart of the matter as indicated by Scripture. God has created man and woman for each other to live in a monogamous union. They are bound together in such a way that they are no longer two but one (6). In view of this unique and exclusive relationship, any breach is unthinkable. It would amount to desecration in the undoing of God's work. Our Lord made no distinction between man and woman in this respect. His prohibition is equally binding on both, although in Jewish law only the man could take the initiative in divorce proceedings.

No place is thus left for the dissolution of a marriage. What then of the Mosaic regulation? Jesus explained that it was a concession to human obduracy. One of the effects of original sin was to petrify not only the feelings but the

15

understanding as well, with the result that man becomes virtually incapable of learning. This, however, was not so before the fall and it cannot therefore be argued that divorce was sanctioned from the beginning (8).

The exceptive clause (9) has been much debated in modern times. There are no grounds for excluding it from the text, as some have done. Although some commentators refer it to pre-marital fornication, it is more likely to apply to adultery. Adultery destroys the very foundations of marriage, although our Lord's alteration of 'command' to 'allow' (7 f.) will surely apply here also. Such divorce (with the possibility of remarriage?) would not be undertaken lightly by a Christian, but our Lord's teaching clearly permits it.

The disciples were clearly astonished at the high standard set by Jesus. They were tempted to wonder whether celibacy was perhaps preferable. But our Lord's teaching implies that marriage is normal for man, although some are called to renounce it for His sake.

## 5 : The Tyranny of the Tongue

### James 3.1–12

After a warning against ambitious over-eagerness to assume the role of a teacher in the church (1), James returns to a theme already introduced in 1.19, 26—namely, the need to control the tongue. He places this discipline in the context of ideal manhood in Christ. Although we are all liable to do wrong, since to err is human, nevertheless, maturity is a goal to be aimed at (2). We are meant to attain the purpose for which we were designed by our Creator and thus to find fulfilment. This involves the discipline not only of the tongue but indeed of the whole person. Such perfection is nothing less than the full realization of the divine likeness (9).

James provides a disturbing insight into our fallen nature as he vividly describes the tyranny of the tongue. He employs three successive illustrations of the truth he is seeking to bring out—that the tongue is the hinge on which man's entire personality turns (3 ff.). If a man can master his tongue, then he can master the rest, just as a rider controls a horse by means of a bit or a helmsman steers a ship even in a gale by means of a rudder. A raging forest fire may be started by a tiny spark and the tongue is similarly dangerous.

The last of these illustrations leads the apostle to enlarge on the menace of the tongue. He begins to mix his colours as he piles one analogy on another. The tongue is a microcosm of wickedness, a spreading stain of pollution, an untamed beast which prowls after its prey, and the venom of a deadly snake. But above all it is a fire—like flames running up all the spokes of a wheel from a burning axle. It sets alight the cycle of existence, fed from hell's own furnace (6 ff.).

James's reference to the image of God occurs in his allusion to the dual use of the tongue, both for blessings and curses. Such an anomaly ought not to be tolerated (10). The seriousness of cursing lies in the fact that it is not only a sin against man but against God. To revile man is to do despite to the image in which he was created. From the Christian standpoint the only safeguard for human dignity is found in the divine Creatorhood.

It is interesting to notice that his language seems to imply that man (despite the fall) is still in some sense in the image of God (cf. 1 Cor. 11.7). Even at his most beastly he is still not a mere animal. God's love in our hearts stirs our compassion towards the lost, and leads us to pray for their recreation in Christ.

### Questions and themes for study and discussion on Studies 1–5

1. In what ways is man akin to the animal creation and in what ways is he superior?

2. How is man's lordship over creation to be expressed today?

3. If a test-tube baby is eventually produced by science, would this invalidate the Christian view of birth?

4. Is the biblical insistence on the indissolubility of marriage intended to apply only to Christians?

5. What other New Testament passages contain warnings against the misuse of speech?

# CHARACTER STUDIES

## 6 : Bathsheba

### 2 Samuel 11

Bathsheba was the daughter of Eliam, probably one of David's Thirty-seven (2 Sam. **23**.34). It was in this context that the brave Uriah met and married her, for the Hittite convert was also one of the chosen Thirty-seven. A romance between a fine soldier and the beautiful daughter of his comrade-in-arms might have run a life-long course of happiness, but for the happenings of one sad afternoon.

Who initiated this historic series of sinful events? It appears from the narrative that it was David looking down from his palace roof on the tangle of houses and courtyards below. But what was Bathsheba doing to be thus visible as she bathed? If she was in full view below, so was David above. From a later appearance in the story, a generation later (1 Kings **1**), it is evident that Bathsheba was a resourceful and clever woman. Nor was David's weakness for women unknown. This is a fault of character which cannot long be hidden. Did the young wife construct the situation? There is more than a suspicion that she spread the net into which David so promptly fell.

Her husband was a fine man. David employed many mercenaries. Men of Cretan stock, no doubt mercenaries from the Philistines, followed him when he retreated before Absalom, and the Hittite, a convert to the worship of Yahweh on the evidence of his name, was one of these strong and trusted men. He was a man of resolution. Observing a taboo which was probably incorporated in the code of the select bodyguard in which he served the king (1 Sam. **21**.4), Uriah was not tricked into a visit to his wife, and the sub-terfuge by which the sinner sought to cover up his sin. Perhaps also Uriah had his suspicions. David had made enquiries (3) about Bathsheba and rumour in an ancient city was not likely to run less fast than rumour runs today.

David himself should have been with his men. But middle-age brought ease. The flatteries of an urban court were undermining his old standards. He grew slack, arrogant, undisciplined, and the Enemy struck at that point in his defences where the victim was weak—an eventuality which is among the sure circumstances of life. He was either the victim of a scheming woman or of his own backsliding. In either case it was an unsanctified corner in his life which provided entrance for the evil which overwhelmed him.

# 7 : Nathan

## 2 Samuel 12

Nathan was a brave man. It was no light matter to face the wrath of an oriental despot, and that is what David had become. Power, as the saying has it, corrupts, and David had power, and used it ill. Courage consists, not in disregarding danger, but in looking danger in the face without flinching. True courage is cool and calm. It is not manifested in brutal force, but in the firm resolve which goodness and reason fortify. It does not imply absence of fear, but fearing the reproach of conscience, the shame of compromise, and the stigma of cowardice, more than the perils of right action. Moral courage, too, is a rarer virtue than physical courage, which is fed by the body's reaction, and often made easier by a blinding of the reason.

By all the tests Nathan was a man of rare courage. He had a task of some magnitude, as well as of danger. He was faced with a psychological and a spiritual problem. David had sought to quench his conscience in action. The attack on the citadel of Rabbah (the modern Amman), which is mentioned at the end of the chapter, probably took place before the events recorded in the first fifteen verses. It may have taken place during Bathsheba's hypocritical mourning for Uriah (11.26 f.). David, like Saul of Tarsus, sought to brain-wash himself by violent action and cruelty (31).

He had a measure of success. Joab, no doubt, did not make it too apparent that he had his uncle in his power. The land at large, which murmured its scorn (14), was remote from the monarch cushioned by his court. A strange numbness of spirit lay upon him. His mind and heart no longer leaped into action, jubilation, or even lamentation, at the touch of circumstance. The poet in him was dead.

After the careful manner of the Hebrew teacher, Nathan approached his task of enlightenment and condemnation with a parable. But such preamble does not preclude the point and the conclusion, and Nathan did not halt short of his solemn duty of firm rebuke. It reached its mark, and broke the sinner down. He was forgiven—but the consequences remained. No sin, as we have observed before, can be confined to the place and time of its committal. The same applies blessedly to every act of good.

## 8: David the Penitent (1)

### Psalm 51.1–17

There is one thing and one only to do with sin, and that is to commit it to God in penitence. If this is done some good can be wrought from it by God's creative hands. Psa. **51**, which has brought comfort and healing to multitudes, was the good which God brought from David's sin.

Psa. **51**, perhaps together with Pss. **32**, **38** and **143**, is David's act of public penitence. It was sung by the Levite choirs, and vs. 18 f, a liturgical addition perhaps from the days of the captivity, are indication that it continued to be sung. Such was the permanence of David's shame, but also of David's repentance and forgiveness. Like Henry the Second, scourged at Becket's tomb eight centuries ago, David let the nation see his sorrow,

The psalm should be studied in all solemnity. If David's carnal sin and sin of blood are not shared by all, he is a fortunate man (or perhaps an insensitive man) who does not feel the kinship of the sinner in more than one verse of this prayer. It is a moving insight into David's mind—his deep sense of sin, the agonizing obsession (3) with his guilt, the sense of uncleanness (2) . . .

He appeals to God's mercy and there is no other plea (1). He makes no excuse. He uses three words for sin, represented by three words in English. First, 'transgression' (1). The Hebrew word means basically 'rebellion'. David was conscious that he had betrayed his God. Second, 'iniquity' (2). Basically the word implies a bending or a twisting of the straight and true. The word 'bent', which C. S. Lewis acquired from George Macdonald, draws near to this conception. Third, 'sin' (3). Like one of the common Greek New Testament words, this word implies a falling short of a goal, a missing of the mark.

Note the plural 'transgressions'. No sin stands alone. 'Wash me,' he calls and the word-picture is deeply embedded in Scripture and Christian ritual (Isa. **1**.16; Jer. **2**.22; **4**.14; Mal. **3**.2). 'My rebellion I recognize,' says v. 3. 'Against THEE, THEE only, have I sinned . . .' (4). He has sinned against Uriah, Bathsheba, Joab and his people, but all this was swallowed up in the thought of God outraged, His love scorned, and His plan cast aside.

And he knew, this man of splendid insight, where it had all begun—in the heart, in evil entertained by the mind (6). It is there that forgiveness, too, must find its base.

## 9 : David the Penitent (2)

### Psalm 32

This theme should not be passed by without further contemplation of the shattered man. Two beatitudes open Psa. **32**. The forgiven sinner is happy, blessed and at peace, because life's greatest problem is solved when a man is reconciled to God.

David had tried to cover his sin, and found it a principle of death in his deepest being (3). God does press hard on the sinner. The fact can be illustrated by the story of Paul, Bunyan, Bilney and Francis Thompson. (Read the vivid lines in *The Hound of Heaven* which begin: 'I fled Him down the nights and down the days'.) 'Give them no rest,' Donald Barnhouse used to pray, 'until they find their rest in Thee' (4). Only surrender brings peace. (Read the last few hundred lines of John Masefield's *Everlasting Mercy*.)

The RSV correctly renders v. 6. The spirit of repentance should not be lost. Such sin as David had committed, as we have seen, can benumb the soul. Amid the storm and turmoil of distress it is sometimes hard to apprehend the truth, and lay hold on God. The image in the verse is of one swept away by a sudden flood. Man needs a refuge (7) from the sting of pursuing conscience, the power, and the doom of sin. Refuges can be false, and of no avail in the stress of the soul (Isa. **28**.15). God alone avails (Isa. **32**.2). No human philosophy, no attenuated and decayed religiosity, can take the place of the living God. 'Thou must save, and Thou alone.'

At v. 8 God takes over the utterance. He promises instruction, direction and guidance—but only to those docile under His hand, and moving willingly according to His will (9).

This is the way of blessedness with which the psalm began. Faith obtains mercy, the theme of **51**.1, mercy which garrisons the soul like a protecting army (10). Joy goes with righteousness, and righteousness is from God (11).

The small psalm contains a wealth of truth and reaches with understanding deep into the New Testament. Go carefully through Psa. **38** in similar fashion. It seems to fit the mood of this time in David's life.

## 10 : David's Household

### 2 Samuel 13; Psalm 143

The chapter is almost too painful to read. Nathan's verdict had been that, though the sin was forgiven, forces were loosed which changed life and changed history. David's example had been ruined. He might well pray that he might show sinners God's way (**51**.13). He was indeed used to 'teach transgressors God's ways', but he also taught transgressors the ways of sin.

Amnon merely did what, in another context, his father had done. So did Absalom, of whom much more will be heard in this disordered household. The whole evil sequence of events began, and ran on, because David had lost his moral hold on his household, and was in no position to rebuke anyone.

From this time, too, begins the political ascendancy of the

brutal and murderous Joab. David had damaged the man's soul by inviting complicity in his sin, and lost, in consequence, any authority which he might have held over him.

Sin is infinitely prolific. Once planted, like some weed, it produces more sin, more unhappiness. Men and women are vastly more important than they imagine. For good or ill, they influence all those with whom they come into contact, and project their sin into other generations—as they also project good.

Psa. **143** seems, by its verbal echoes, to belong to this period of David's life, perhaps a little later in time than the cry of penitential agony of Psa. **51**. It is more positive in its outlook, and sees the issues of righteousness with sharper clarity. The prayer of everyone should be in the words of vs. 6, 8, 9, 10. There should be a conscious reaching after God and good. 'If with all your hearts, ye truly seek me . . .' says Jer. **29**.13 in the famous choral rendering, and no blessing attends half-hearted seeking. Trust is a 'lifting up of the soul' in such an eager quest, a retreat into God, and above all, a life-long preoccupation with God's will. Such was the wisdom which David learned in the school of his own self-inflicted catastrophe. He set it down in poetry and song, that others might learn from schooling less harsh and grievous. This was the one good he could snatch for God from calamitous events. For himself he moved on to face what might be. His enlightenment had increased the burden of his responsibility.

### Questions and themes for study and discussion on Studies 6–10

1. 'No one ever became suddenly bad' (Juvenal).

2. What does repentance imply?

3. The heart as the fount out of which sinful acts flow.

4. The influence of sin upon others.

# MAN AND SIN

## Fallen: The Genesis Record

### 11 : The Fall of Man

#### Genesis 3.1-7

So far we have been looking at man as he was in creation. Clearly this is not how he now is. How did he become otherwise? The Bible simply says that he fell. He lapsed from his original state of innocence. Nothing less than a major catastrophe affecting the whole of his personality is sufficient to account for man's present alienation and misery. Even modern philosophers like Heidegger resort to the categories of 'falling' and 'thrownness', though not, of course, with theological overtones.

The impulse to sin, according to the biblical account, came from outside man. Nothing in nature as given by God compelled him to fall. Yet it is equally evident that man is held responsible for his own defection. Even though the first human sin was induced by the tempter, it is regarded nevertheless as a wilful self-corruption on the part of its perpetrator.

The essence of the fall lay in disobedience. God's prohibition was sufficiently categorical (2.16 f.). The fatal stages which led up to the sinful act are traced in this chapter. Here is how man still succumbs. It began with doubting God's word (1). 'Did God say?'—according to F. Delitzsch 'a half-interrogatory, half-exclamatory expression of astonishment,' as if the serpent had brooded for a long time over the paradox and had eventually reached a reluctantly critical conclusion. When the woman had repudiated the serpent's distortion of the divine command—even over-correcting it with a proviso of her own (3)—the tempter threw aside insinuation and came out with a flat denial (4). Then he impugned God's motives by slyly suggesting that He wanted to keep man down lest His own prerogatives should be

24

threatened. This unworthy charge was utterly groundless, for God's decree was designed only for man's good. Yet it contains the kernel of sin, which is the attempt to become like God (or 'gods', NEB). The titanism which aspired to usurp the Almighty power and wisdom brought about man's downfall. He wanted to become a law to himself. In his vaulting ambition he snatched at what belonged to God alone. Hence William of Sens confessed in Dorothy Sayer's play *The Zeal of Thy House* that he had been struck down by 'the eldest sin of all'—the pride that thinks it can play God.

Human eyes were now opened (5, 7) and immediately the spell of innocence was broken. Because he grasped what was forbidden, man has ever since experienced a 'longing which cannot be stilled' (E. Brunner).

*Meditation : The first sin was conceived in mistrust. What about my sins? Do they often begin there?*

## 12 : Results of the Fall

### Genesis 3.8–20

The immediate consequences of the fall are described in v. 7. It brought with it an awareness of sin's seriousness and a profoundly disturbing sense of shame. The feeling was at once the outcome of sin and a reaction against it.

In the interview with God that follows from v. 8 onwards an enquiry is conducted (9–13) and the sentences are pronounced (14–19). Man's communion with his Maker was impaired by his disobedience (8). It was not that God withdrew His presence. He appeared as before in the garden—the place of fellowship. But on hearing the rustle of His footsteps—His approach can only be indicated in such anthropomorphic terms—the guilty pair tried to conceal themselves. Avoidance of God was a further result of the fall. It is all the more tragic in that the One from whom they shrank was still reaching out to them in love. 'It was God their Creator who now, as God the Redeemer was seeking the lost' (Delitzsch).

God not only came but called (9). In grace He sought to elicit a response from man the sinner. Even when thus summoned the man multiplied excuses. The old confidence was broken. No wonder Luther commented that Adam was now totally changed to become another man. With the instinctive craftiness of an evil conscience he sidestepped responsibility by blaming his wife. The infection spread as the woman in turn blamed the serpent. Suddenly something was rotten in the state of Eden, as in Hamlet's Denmark. The knowledge of good and evil had spoiled man's original relationship with God. The key to man's fallen condition is to be found in v. 10: 'I was afraid.' As the psychologists confirm, fear invariably lies at the root of man's malaise.

The penalties imposed first on the serpent and then on Eve and Adam represent further consequences of the fall. The hostility between Satan and man brings in its train hatred, violence, oppression and strife (15). In the case of the woman sexual life is now accompanied by the labour pains of childbirth and the dominance of the male threatens to reduce her to subjugation. In the case of the man, work which had formerly been a delight now becomes a burden. For both, death waits at the end as 'a kind of sacrament of sin' (J. Denney).

*A Thought: In blaming another I often reveal that I am a Child of the Fall. Grace enables me to face up to moral reality.*


## 13 : Paradise Lost

### Genesis 3.22–4.16

As soon as he became a sinner, man was ejected from the garden of Eden and excluded from the tree of life (3.23 f.). This banishment, enforced by the divine decree, was a logical necessity. Partaking of the tree symbolized eternal fellowship with God, for eternal life is knowing God (John 17.3). This was man's destiny at his creation. Probably, after a period of probation, he would be raised to the status of permanent sonship. But sin had now intervened. Man had chosen the

26

way of death rather than the way of life. That decision was humanly speaking irrevocable. The return route is not merely difficult: it is altogether impossible to man, however much he may desire it. The flashing sword turns 'every way' in its comprehensive circular motion (24). If man is ever to find eternal life it will be by the sheer undeserved grace of God.

If Gen. 3 records the first human sin against God, Gen. 4 records the first sin of man against man. Of course, since man is made in the image of God, it is also a sin against God, for that is always the nature of sin (Psa. 51.4). When Cain's gift was rejected his reaction was one of resentment and dejection (5). God's probing question 'Why?' (cf. 'Where?' in Gen. 3.9) led to a solemn warning against the seduction of sin. In a vivid metaphor sin is depicted as a wild beast crouching in readiness to leap on its prey (7, cf. 1 Pet. 5.8). If Cain failed to master it, then it would master him. Sin is recognized as an objective force against man.

The murder of Abel appears as deliberate and cold-blooded. Cain invited his brother to go with him into the solitude of the open country where the crime would be unobserved (8). 'Human sin made a gigantic advance in this act' (Delitzsch). 'Where?' reappeared (cf. 3.9) as a social question (9). Cain's truculent reply suggests the hardening of sin.

The full weight of sin's offence is brought home as Cain cried out in his anguish (13). As von Rad puts it, he realized that a life far from God is a life He no longer protects. But the final word is with mercy as he received a promise of immunity from the blood avenger.

*Meditation: If God has graciously reconciled me to Himself, to what extent has this affected my relations with other people? (cf. Eph. 2.14-18; 1 John 2.9-11).*


## 4 : Universal Corruption

### Genesis 6.1–22

The enigmatic narrative about the origin of the Nephilim (1-4) is apparently introduced to account in part for the further corruption of mankind prior to the flood. As D.

27

Kidner suggests, however the passage is interpreted a new stage has been reached in the progress of evil, and man is seen to be beyond self-help.

A more emphatic and all-embracing assertion of human wickedness than is contained in v. 5 could scarcely be imagined. Its magnitude, its inwardness, its comprehensiveness, its continuity and its monotonous invariability are all alluded to. The effect on God of this pervasive depravity is indicated in v. 6. The purposes of grace seemed to be frustrated and God even began to regret that He had ever created man. He was so deeply grieved that He resolved on the destruction of the world (7). Here we see what sin means to God, and only as we realize how it appears in His sight do we begin to grasp the full extent of its enormity.

This devastating account of universal corruption is confirmed in vs. 11 f. The repetitions hammer home the grim fact. The earth was now filled with violence—arbitrary, anarchistic oppression and the elemental breach of law and order (11). The whole of mankind had deliberately involved itself in defection (12). Responsibility for this catastrophic state of affairs is firmly placed on man's own shoulders.

All this is strikingly, almost frighteningly, modern. Sin in society is not static, but is an ugly dynamic, a kind of active leaven affecting the whole lump. Societies do not move nearer righteousness but further away from it unless God brings a 'wind of change' towards Him by the Spirit of His grace in Christ. The unnatural sex (if the 'sons of God' are fallen angels, as many commentators think) and the plenitude of violence make us think of our own day.

There was, however, one exception to this otherwise unanimous indictment. Righteous Noah found favour in the sight of the God with whom he walked in fellowship and was chosen to be the pioneer of a new generation. But apart from Noah and his family no one was to be spared. God had determined to do away with the rest. 'End' (13) is a common term in later eschatology in connection with divine judgement. On the inclusiveness of the punishment depends the inclusiveness of the salvation foreshadowed by the ark.

*A Thought: If our intercession for such a world is to reach the heavenly Throne we need first to view the world as God does and to acknowledge that we are ourselves 'debtors to mercy alone'.*

## Questions and themes for study and discussion on Studies 11–14

1. Evolutionary anthropologists appear to see only a 'rise' where the Bible speaks of a fall. What arguments can be advanced in support of the Christian view of man as fallen?

2. Consider Gen. 3.1–7 in the light of 1 Tim. 2.13 f. Is Paul really placing most of the blame on Eve, as is sometimes assumed?

3. How does Gen. 3.14–19 help us to understand the world in which we live?

4. Ponder the comments on Gen. 4 in Heb. 11.4 and 1 John 3.11 ff.

5. In what ways does the account of universal corruption before the flood find its counterpart in the modern world?

# CHARACTER STUDIES

## 15 : Absalom

### 2 Samuel 13

This chapter is almost too horrible to read, but the Bible does not profess to be anything but a record of the truth, and it is bitter truth that evil was abroad in David's family. Of poor Tamar and the vile Amnon nothing need be said. Of Absalom, scourge of his father, much will be heard. In passion and in violence he enters the story; in passion and in violence he will leave it.

The roots of the evil which clustered round the prince went back deep into the past. Absalom should never have been born. To the north-west, on the edge of the desert along the road to Damascus, lay the sheikdom of Geshur. The wider conquests of David thrust far in that direction, and it was part of his settlement of the frontiers to cement buffer-areas by dynastic ties with the border princelings. This is no doubt the background of David's alliance in marriage with Maacah, the daughter of Geshur's ruler (2 Sam. 3.3).

We have already marked a fundamental fault in David's character, for which he paid dearly. It must have been a wilful fault. He knew enough of the old laws of his land to be well aware of ancient prohibitions against intermingling with pagans. He was also an enlightened man. The early psalms show deep awareness of God's ways, and reveal his own deep yearning to stand well with God. But David was a man of strong passions, polygamy was sanctioned, the alliance was necessary, and there was abundant motive and excuse for following the desires of the flesh. Maacah, probably beautiful, and passionate in her Bedouin way, was the king's temptation. And thus he fathered Absalom, misnamed Father of Peace, and so brought strife and bitter grief into his house.

For some unrevealed reason, perhaps for his wild mother's sake, David loved Absalom with unreasoning blindness. It is with some horror that the reader realizes, as the chapter closes, that the son for whom David mourns (37) is not the dead Amnon, but the living refugee, Absalom. It may well be imagined in what sort of an atmosphere the undisciplined young man had grown up. He was probably denied no wish or whim. He could hate fiercely. He could plot and hold his tongue. He was savagely proud. The wrong done to his sister touched his honour, and revenge was part of his mother's desert code. And Absalom was his mother's son.

# 16 : Absalom's Father

## Deuteronomy 8.11–14; John 15.1–6; Revelation 2.4, 5, 21–23

It is not true that parents are always to blame for the sins of their children, but it is a charge not to be denied in too many cases for our comfort. This point in the narrative cannot be passed without a glance at the condition of Absalom's father. Hence the readings on back-sliding, especially relevant to those of David's age and condition—successful, beginning to age, and a prey to that erosion of stern standards and weakening ideals which once tautened and sustained the spirit.

A grim picture of the royal court emerges from these chapters in the story. A household is so often what the head, by example or permissiveness, makes it. The court is a scene familiar to history, of mishandled affluence, power misused and abused, of suspicion, hatred and intrigue. The head of the household, unchallenged in the place of power, seemingly secure, had sadly deteriorated. The old hero of the people, the dashing guerrilla chief, able to win the love and devotion of men, the object of ready loyalty and self-sacrifice, had become the aloof and self-centred despot, the victim, as such men often are, of the military men and the women around him.

And what of his own record of tyranny? The court knew, the people knew, of Uriah and Bathsheba. In agony and contrition, that dual sin had been put right with God, but human malice, ever ready to bring down the proud, the uplifted, and the good, laid hold of the sin, and forgot the repentance. Nor was the attitude of the people at large entirely dictated by malice. Justice was a deep-seated passion in Israel. The Decalogue, too, was known in every home. David had trampled on two commandments, and scorned a third. He had been a great leader, but leadership depends on moral worth, and there were those who could no longer believe in David's moral worth. The old days of strife, through which David's military genius had forged a united Israel, were receding into history. A new generation was rising, and tribal sin was rearing its divided head. It is common enough with the young to question established authority, especially when those who carry it forfeit the reverence upon which all authority must ultimately rest. David is a sorry sight, backslidden, falsely secure, obstinate, deceived—and about to be dealt with by the God he had known, and had so sadly forgotten.

## 17 : Absalom's Return

### 2 Samuel 14.1–15.12

The lamentable state of David's rule is evident in this story. He was weak, but obviously difficult to deal with and approach. Joab's subterfuge shows how the king had lost touch with his subjects and how incalculable his moods were. Absalom was allowed to return to Jerusalem with neither rebuke nor punishment.

'Not so had God taught David to forgive', runs a footnote in Dr. Scofield's well-known annotated Bible. 'It would seem,' he continues 'that had David at this time taken Absalom into intimacy, the rebellion might have been averted.' Few will agree with this view. Absalom deserved chastisement. He had murdered a brother, and gave no sign of repentance. Amnon, to be sure, had richly earned his fate, but royal authority, under royal law, should have exacted some satisfaction and requital.

David would have precipitated rebellion from some other quarter had Absalom been promoted to any sort of intimacy. The best fate would have been to leave him in his self-imposed exile. But in the whole incident, David's moral torpor is evident. It is the same mood as that in which Nathan found him after his great sin, dull and insensitive.

Absalom waited, obviously expecting some move from the palace. Seeing no intention either to chastise or to restore him, he began audaciously to plot under the very eyes of the languid king. He set himself up in ostentatious state, and impudently set out to win the affections of his own generation, and of the rebellious and disgruntled among the people. It is impossible to imagine that no one brought such treason to the notice of the king. Perhaps the spirit of revolt lapped the very palace, or perhaps David was quite unable to believe such enormities about his pampered son.

A sort of paralysis lay upon him, as the land seethed. Older men in Israel would be wary of the young demagogue, but younger men found him attractive, and in a land where justice lacked adequate machinery (15.2–6), and the ruler, who should have dispensed justice, grew remote, there would be a host who nursed grievance, who desired change, or who saw advantage in revolt. They cohered round the young rebel.

# 18 : David's Flight

## 2 Samuel 15.7–37; Psalm 2

It required a shock to bring David back to life. The shock, in the mercy of God, came. It was to give a spiritually moribund man a new lease of life. Taking advantage of a religious festival in the old royal capital of Hebron, Absalom had himself proclaimed king. It was a piece of audacity in keeping with his wild, flamboyant character. Hebron is a bare twenty miles south of Jerusalem, along the land's central spine of hills, and the news must have reached the king in a matter of hours.

It galvanized him to life. In a moment he assessed the military situation. All the old warrior instincts in him revived. The wilderness was always a symbol of security in Hebrew thought. David had proved its reality over long years. The city was a trap. In the desert was hope. With bitter clarity David saw that Jerusalem was a snare. A guerrilla fighter must, as we have seen, have the countryside with him. Towns are his ruin. The choices, at that critical moment, were plain. It was obviously a matter of retreat in one of three directions. First, there was the coastal plain where the old Philistine foe offered small security. Second, there was the way north, where tribal disaffection lay. Since Absalom lay across the southern route, the only way left was down to the Jordan valley, and across to Mahanaim. This involved a tactical manoeuvre of great peril, a retreat across the front of the enemy. It reveals David's renewed vigour of mind that he saw, in swift decisiveness, that this is what he had to do.

He was a new man. The smell of the hot rocks and the sand of the old wilderness was in his nostrils. He was ready to trust God and risk all on firm, swift action. Perhaps Psa. **2** reflects one apprehension which he had to face. The border tribes had been subdued in David's wide stabilization of his borderlands. They would hear of dynamic strife in Israel, and be ready for advantage. On this issue David could only trust God. The raging heathen and the people of Israel, seduced by vain promises, both found a place in that psalm of confidence, and the verse reflects a new-born faith.

The little army crossed the Kedron and bore east. There were faithful mercenaries, some of them Philistines—the Cherethites and the men from Gath. Ittai the Gittite was such a man as David had destroyed in Uriah. And Ittai recognized a new David, or perhaps the old David come back to life.


## 19 : Shimei

### 2 Samuel 16

For a fearfully dangerous hour or two the column wound out of Jerusalem, over the Mount of Olives, and on to the long descent of the Jericho road. They intended to swing north-east from that long highway and make for the Jordan wilderness by a higher route. But this was Absalom's moment, and he cannot have lacked supporters to advise an immediate attack. Bemused by his own royal splendour and what he imagined victory, Absalom, the victim of his own arrogance, made for Jerusalem. David's column of refugees, travelling slowly with women and children, can have been hardly more than ten miles away.

Had David needed a demonstration that, even in the capital, the people were not all with him, Shimei provided it. Shimei stood for the house of Saul, whom David had displaced. The day of trouble brings out the hidden evil in a situation, and David was subject to abuse, in which he recognized some ring of truth, at his own city gate. It left its mark on his mind, as Psalm 3 reveals. On the level of human judgement, David had the blood of base murder on his conscience. The crude calumnies of Shimei were not without justification, but took no account of David's penitence, which was public enough.

Shimei himself is revealed in the act. Slander is the revenge of a coward. David dealt with it well. The way to check slander is to treat it with contempt. Try to overtake it, and it outruns the pursuer. David treated Shimei with grace, though the man must have been a burden to bear as he followed the small band on the other side of the Kedron ravine, shouting his curses, and throwing stones. So the king left his royal city.

But they had not been intercepted on the Mount of Olives, 'close thing' though it was, with Absalom on their right flank moving up from Hebron. It was of the utmost urgency to press on. It was beyond belief to every experienced soldier there that no cloud of dust rose down the road to Bethlehem and Hebron. They staggered on as fast as they dared, chose a camping-place, and bivouacked for the night. They slept, and woke, and the moods and trepidations of the next few days seem to be reflected in a handful of psalms which tell us much of David's character. Meanwhile Absalom and the scoundrel Ahithophel entered Jerusalem. It was a fatal blunder.

# 20 : Hushai

## 2 Samuel 17.1–22

Hushai was a loyal man, and it is all to his credit that Absalom was surprised to see him apparently throwing in his lot with the godless crew he had gathered round him. By the rough rules of warfare, Hushai's subtle part was a necessary one. He was fighting Absalom with the weapons which the dissolute prince himself had chosen. Absalom could ask no more. He had brought treachery and deceit to the contest. Treachery and deceit were to be the final cause of his failure.

Ahithophel's plan was the only militarily feasible one. David needed time to withdraw to his old guerrilla strongholds. A swift attack by a fast-moving body of chosen troops alone could prevent him and finish the war. Villain though he was, Ahithophel saw this with blinding clarity, and when his advice was rejected he knew with such conviction that the rebel cause was doomed that suicide seemed to him the only resource.

Hushai understood Absalom well. He had marked his delusions of grandeur. He played upon his pathological vanity, and led him to picture himself glittering in armour at the head of a united Israel, gathered from Dan to Beersheba, to sweep the king away (12 f.). It was subtle counsel, and psychologically sound, but somehow Hushai's role seems an ignoble one. His trickery of Absalom involved lying deceit. It involved taking the name of God in vain (16.18). At the same time it involved no little courage. The deep and difficult question is how far a good and salutary end can justify the means, and to what extent any follower of any cause can be sure that the end in view is, in God's eyes, good and salutary.

Hushai, having played his dangerous and difficult part, disappears from the page of history. Absalom appears to have had some inkling of a plot and almost apprehended the two priests who acted as Hushai's messengers. Did he discover Hushai's part, and did the brave friend of David pay with his life for the mission he undertook in Jerusalem?

Meanwhile the days passed. Hastened by Hushai's information, the royal party pushed north-east towards the Jordan. Pss. 3 to 6 seem to reflect these days. The heading of the first of the four is old and traditional. The rest seem to follow in a morning, evening sequence.


## 21 : Ahithophel

### Psalm 41; John 13

Part of the interest of David's story lies in the abundance of material in the psalms which flowed from his poet's pen in moments of stress, or of gladness. We can read of dire events in the historical record, and then turn to observe their sharp reflection in the one who suffered under them.

Many psalms have no traditional heading, and the identification of event and utterance must often be a matter of conjecture. Allow this, and a fruitful area of study opens. We have read Psa. **41** following the chapter on Ahithophel's betrayal because it seems clearly to reflect David's reaction to his courtier's treachery (9). David had a great capacity for friendship, and people who thus give themselves react strongly to disloyalty. Treachery is one of the most detestable vices in the catalogue of human baseness. It is compounded of deceit, self-seeking, cowardice and revenge.

David's reaction was shocked grief. Perhaps these words took shape in his mind during the retreat to Jordan and Mahanaim when he seems to have written Pss. **2**, **3**, **4**, **5** and **6**. David had learned one of life's greatest lessons—that anything, even the grimmest evil, committed to God can be transformed into good. The sordid act of a renegade had hurt him to the heart. A base man had played him false. David handed the whole sorry packet of wickedness and pain to God, and turned it into prayer and poetry.

The result? The experience, like the other experience of pain, whatever it was which lay behind Psa. **22**, broke out of the transient into the eternal. The words became prophecy and found a place in the greater pain of Christ, the Son after the flesh of Israel's king (John **13**.18 f.).

Read Psa. **41** with care, and see pain turn into praise. David is 'poor' (1), and not only in material things. In a moving passage in his commentary on Isaiah, George Adam Smith shows how, from the prophets to the Sermon on the Mount and the Epistle of James, the 'poor' in the Bible, which is an Eastern book, are the deprived, the dispossessed, the victims of injustice, the stripped of privilege. David, in this sad moment, was all of this. And so Ahithophel, already judged, though David did not know it, inspired a psalm.

## Questions and themes for study and discussion on Studies 15–21

1. 'The roots of most evil go deep into the past'.

2. Backsliding—definition, incidence, and cure.

3. The prerequisites of forgiveness.

4. How should a Christian deal with abuse, insult and slander?

5. Could a Christian be a spy?

6. Are lies ever justified?

7. How do we 'commit' pain to God?

# MAN AND SIN

## Fallen: In Psalms and Wisdom Literature

### 22 : Sin and Suffering

#### Psalm 38

This is the prayer of a repentant and chastened sinner. It is the third of the penitential psalms and designed to accompany a memorial offering (Lev. 2.1–10; 24.7). It is traditionally ascribed to David and although there is no direct hint as to the occasion, it is assumed that like Psa. 51 it has the king's adultery as its background. He is troubled in body, mind and soul. He is afflicted by a sickness which he recognizes as in some way associated with his sin. The reasons for his suffering are listed: 'because of thy indignation' (3), 'because of my sin' (3), 'because of my foolishness' (5).

There is no attempt to gloss over the seriousness of sin. The psalmist feels like a man in danger of drowning. His iniquities overwhelm him with the pressure of waves in flood (4). He sees his sin as folly (5b). He has played the fool, and his stupidity is all the more irresponsible because it is self-destructive. Sin has deprived him of joy: life is a misery and he goes about in black like one bereaved (6). He is 'all battered and benumbed' (NEB) and the wild surging of his heart makes him growl like a lion in pain (8). What sin pays out is death (Rom. 6.23) and the distribution begins even in life. Sin, suffering and wrath are all inter-related, although suffering may not necessarily be the result of a man's own wrongdoing.

The psalm contains three distinct appeals to God's mercy (1, 9, 15.). The recognition that chastisement is inflicted by God brings with it the assurance that it will not prove too hard to bear and that relief and restoration will follow. God's arrows have been aimed at the psalmist and God's hand has pressed down heavily on him (2). His plight is known to the Lord who hears his sighs (9). Hence he can confidently commit his cause to God and fix his hope on Him (15). The Lord will answer with forgiveness.

The psalmist concludes with a frank confession. His foot often slips (16). He is always liable to fall headlong, for he is incapable of standing firm in his own strength. He cannot escape from the consciousness of his guilt: godly sorrow for sin is his constant companion. He freely admits his iniquity and makes no secret of it. His is the repentance of faith which despairs of itself but not of God.

What can we learn from all this? Job's comforters were wrong when they dealt with Job on the assumption that his sickness was the result of some awful and specific sin in his own life. Nevertheless, the modern doctor and psychiatrist have plenty of experience of ailments which have their source in the sufferer's own wrongdoing. To any such this psalm presents a case to face reality—the ugly reality of sin and the glorious reality of the forgiveness God offers to the truly penitent. In such circumstances we can identify ourselves with the prayers of the psalmist and find that his God has not changed.


## 23 : Confession

### Psalm 51

In this the most penetrating of all the penitential psalms 'the uttermost depth of sin is grasped' (A. Weiser). The title relates the confession to David's acceptance of Nathan's rebuke after he had seduced Bathsheba and disposed of Uriah. It is an amplification of his acknowledgement: 'I have sinned against the Lord' (2 Sam. **12**.13). There is no attempt to present a defence or to plead extenuating circumstances. Nor is there any appeal to previous righteousness as counterbalancing current guilt. The single-heartedness of David's confession reveals how completely his mind is dominated by the realization of his sin. The urgency and intensity of his pleas, coupled with the reiteration of the same expressions of contrition, indicate the depth and genuineness of his repentance.

He speaks of transgressions in the plural (1, 3), for his offences had multiplied. No sin ever stands alone. One invariably leads to another and even more. Nothing breeds so quickly as sin. Sin is here identified in terms of departure from the norm (transgression, vs. 1, 3), deflection from the ideal (sin, vs. 2, 3, 5), perversion of the right (iniquity, vs. 2, 5), and displeasing God (evil, v. 4). It is a debt to be cancelled or a record to be expunged (9), a stain to be removed with a detergent, and a disease to be cured by medication (7).

It is recognized as an inherited bias, but this is not allowed to degenerate into an excuse (5). The fact that the tendency to sin is innate does not relieve man of responsibility for the sins he willingly makes his own. Incidentally, we have here 'such a clear confession of original sin . . . . . that the spiritual affinity with Genesis 3 is incontestable,' according to Eichrodt. As he puts it, we have no need to go into 'exegetical wriggles' to evade this insight.

The psalmist realizes that although he has sinned grievously against others, his real offence is against God (4, cf. Gen. **39**.9). The corollary of this recognition is that only God can relieve man of his guilt. Our society is sick because it fails to act on the implications of this truth.

## 24 : Moral Imperfection

### Proverbs 20.1–22

From ch. **16** onwards the writer of Proverbs assumes the existence of personal sins as distinct from national defection. The forms which such transgressions may take are varied. Amongst those catalogued here are intemperance (1), anger (2, cf. **19**.12), contention (3), idleness (4, 13), fraud (10, 14, 17), gossip (19), disrespect for parents (20), greed (21), and revenge (22).

The possibility of an upright life is by no means ruled out. Indeed, it is set up as an ideal to be cherished (7). Nevertheless, while there are many who claim to be trustworthy, yet few pass the test (6). Profession is common; fulfilment is rare. So often offers of help prove hollow. It is not easy to find someone who can really be relied on in a time of crisis. Such is the fallibility of human nature that good intentions are seldom translated into corresponding acts. Man often means well but fails to do well. The final test is action (11).

Hence the admission of universal failure in v. 9, which

Eichrodt considers to have been accepted at this period as an axiom of belief. Who indeed can claim to have a completely clear conscience and to be purified from every stain of sin (cf. Job **15**.14)? This declaration of man's moral imperfection was evidently the outcome of observation and reflection. The terms used here make it obvious that the reference is to moral and not to ceremonial uncleanness. Later Jewish teaching would claim that the attainment of moral perfection is the only means of getting right with God. In Ecclesiasticus **3**.14f. a son's fulfilment of his duty towards his father in old age is said to be entered in the credit column of the ledger to counterbalance sins which because of this will melt like frost in the sun. No such scheme of salvation by works is in evidence here in Proverbs, nor, indeed, any hint that man is capable of producing righteousness at will.

*A thought: In the New Testament one word does service for the two ideas 'faith' and 'faithfulness'. If I am to be trustworthy my life must be grounded by faith on Him who is faithful.*

## 25 : The Emptiness of Life

### Ecclesiastes 1.1–18

The theme of Ecclesiastes is announced in v. 2. The author appears to state his conclusion at the outset as well as at the close (**12**.8). It is found no less than thirty-nine times altogether in the book. Here it is to be regarded as a proposition rather than a verdict. What follows in the successive chapters of Ecclesiastes is the evidence gathered largely from the Speaker's own experience. All human existence divorced from God is utterly frustrating and unsatisfying. Man out of touch with his Maker can never sort out the meaning of life or achieve integration and happiness.

It must be realized that the Speaker (*qôhelet,* the president of the assembly) is considering human experience from a purely this-worldly, materialistic standpoint. Omit the spiritual dimension and what does it look like? His perspective is 'under the sun' (14). This phrase recurs again and again (29 times) to remind us that the author writes within self-imposed limitations. As, like space-age man, he searches for significance in 'all that is done under heaven' (13) he makes no reference to divine revelation. Can it be then that he is deliberately endeavouring to demonstrate man's total inability to solve the mystery of life apart from the light God gives? He is not an unqualified pessimist, as it might seem. His pessimism is confined to the prospects of disorientated man.

To man out of relation to God life presents itself as a wearisome cycle (3–11). There is a desolating sameness about it. It is rather like the headlines of the news today—the names and places change but what happens is sickeningly similar. Is life really getting anywhere? Because of this disenchantment man feels that all his energies are being wasted (3).

From v. 12 the Speaker begins to draw specifically from his own experience. He was noted as a seeker after wisdom. But at the end of all his investigations he decides that life is 'a sorry business' (13 NEB). He has only been chasing the wind (14, 17). More knowledge only brings more sorrow.

How modern all this seems! Novels, plays, films, poetry, painting, music—so much in all the art-forms of today combines to present us with one doleful message: everything is without meaning! And so it is—without Christ!

## 26 : Broken Cisterns

### Ecclesiastes 2.1–11

Like the rich man in Luke 12.18 f. the Speaker has a conversation with himself once more (cf. 1.16). He will try a further experiment. Instead of applying himself to philosophy, he will discover whether pleasure can bring him satisfaction. 'Enjoy yourself' is the motto of the worldly man. What does he get out of it? The answer is precisely nothing (1). He decides that laughter borders on madness, even controlled hedonism is futile, and the stimulus of alcohol is abortive (2 f.). How much more the uncontrolled hedonism of our permissive age!

Next he turns to culture in order to fulfil his creative instinct (4–6). There is a parallel to his experiment in Tennyson's *Palace of Art*, with the same unsatisfactory outcome. The quest for beauty and the aesthetic comforts of gracious living are incapable of meeting man's profoundest needs. The creature cannot be content with the creation. He requires the Creator too. Behind all forms he must find the reality.

In vs. 7–11 the Speaker relates how he acquired possessions in the hope that they might afford him satisfaction. The acquisitive instinct is inherent in man. The communist philosophy denies something that is basic to human life. The urge to possess is not in itself necessarily iniquitous; it may be no more than a collector's mania. But it can never bring ultimate fulfilment, and may easily get out of hand and degenerate into an obsession. The Speaker amassed wealth and with it all that wealth can provide. He owned land and property. His flocks and herds were larger than those of any of his predecessors (7b). He had a staff of household slaves to wait on him (7a). Singers of both sexes supplied music, whilst his harem was filled with concubines (if that indeed is the meaning of an uncertain Hebrew phrase in v. 8). No effort was spared to indulge his passion to possess. Yet when he adds it all up, it only amounts to emptiness and chasing the wind (11). No surplus swells his credit. What a rebuke to our materialistic age! The desire of the underprivileged for material things is understandable, but what shall we say of the mad pursuit of wealth and possessions by those who already have too much for happiness, but who are not 'rich toward God'? A man may gain the whole world and yet forfeit his life (Matt. **16**.26).

## 27 : Wisdom and Work

### Ecclesiastes 2.12–26

The Speaker reports another stage in his search for happiness. Pleasure, culture and wealth have failed to satisfy him. Now he returns to his search for wisdom (12–17, cf. **1**.17). It is noticeable that this had never been abandoned altogether. In his pursuit of pleasure and wealth, he allowed wisdom to be his guide (**2**.3, 9). Now he accords it priority.

He recognizes that it has its undoubted value, for light is preferable to darkness (13). He quotes what is evidently a proverb to the effect that the wise man sees ahead whereas the fool is content to grope in the dark (14). Even though this may be so, the same fate awaits all at the end (16, cf. Heb. 9.27). Death is the great leveller and both the wise and the foolish will be claimed by the grave. The same thought is found in Psa. **49**.10 and Job **21**.26. There is moreover no special remembrance of the wise, and as time passes everything will be lost in oblivion. These sombre if not cynical observations lead to an extreme revulsion from existence itself (cf. 2 Sam. **13**.15; Isa. **1**.14; Amos **5**.21).

That is an attitude with which we are all too familiar today. Our society has sunk below the despair line, as Kierkegaard put it. There is a widespread disenchantment with life. It would seem that the only logical outcome is suicide and it is an escape route which is increasingly used. But most are deterred by the undefined fear of Hamlet's 'something after death'. They still cling to life even whilst they are pronouncing it hateful.

In vs. 18–23 the Speaker considers yet another area which might give him the satisfaction he seeks. Perhaps work will provide the answer. But he declares himself to be disillusioned about the merits of honest toil. Of what profit is it if after all his efforts he will have to leave his business to someone who has not deserved it and may not appreciate or develop it (18 f.)? The thought is enough to drive him to despair (20). So he concludes that only as God is seen in work and wisdom can they bring any satisfaction. There is no ultimate contentment apart from Him. 'He is the substitute for everything. Nothing can be a substitute for Him' (C. Bridges).

## 28 : The Folly of Folly

### Ecclesiastes 10.1–20

The section from **9**.17 to **10**.20 contains a collection of proverbial sayings about wise men and fools—a recurring theme in Ecclesiastes. Even a little folly spoils the effect of wisdom, just as dead flies turn the perfumer's ointment rancid. The analogy reminds us of Paul's allusion to the leaven in the dough (1 Cor. **5**.6). The fool in Scripture is the man who disdains moral principles and lives as a practical

45

atheist. This kind of folly is far from dead. The particular word employed here in Ecclesiastes (*sakal*) implies an almost irrational obtuseness. Even a modicum of such an attitude can blight the whole character. It will determine not only the direction we face in life (2), but also our ultimate destiny (cf. Matt. **25**.31–46).

The Speaker proceeds to deplore the incidence of folly in high places (4–7). It can do untold harm. Its effect is to disturb the settled order of society. The revolutionary spirit displaces the natural rulers of men and reverses the normal roles (6 f.). It was the habit of tyrants to promote the base-born to positions of honour. To ride on horseback was usually the prerogative of the aristocracy. The Roman historian Justin explained that this was how freemen were distinguished from slaves amongst the Parthians. Cf. Esther **6**.8 f. But when the social order is overturned and it is the slaves who commandeer the horses whilst princes go on foot, anarchy threatens the welfare of the realm.

Verses 8–15 contrast the advantages of wisdom with the consequences of folly. Even in the practical matters of man's everyday occupation it is better to use discretion. Folly produces its own friction which increases the burden of work. In v. 16 the Speaker issues a warning against evil rulers. It is a tragedy for any country when a slave (NEB) has been thrust on the throne and his advisers begin the day with revelry instead of administering the affairs of state (cf. Isa. **5**.11).

Such teaching needs to be weighed carefully. Does it mean that the social order should be taken as fixed for all time? Was Wilberforce wrong in pressing for the emancipation of the slaves, and treating this as a matter of Christian concern? Is the writer's perspective a purely worldly one —given to us through inspiration as a warning of worldly vanity—which would have to be modified considerably in the light of other parts of Scripture and, perhaps, of the conclusion of his own book? It is well worth giving some thought to this matter.

## Questions and themes for study and discussion on Studies 22–28

1. What does the Bible teach about the relationship between sin and disease?

2. How can man be held responsible for his sins if sin is an inborn tendency?

3. Is there any trace of the outlook of Ecclesiastes in the New Testament?

4. If modern secular man has succumbed to despair, how may the message of Christian hope be most effectively presented to him?

5. On the whole, contemporary man would feel more kinship with the writer of Ecclesiastes than did the European or American of the 19th century. Why?

# CHARACTER STUDIES

## 29 : David and His Foes

### Psalm 2; Ephesians 6.10–20

Psa. 2 breaks out of time into the eternal, and the New Testament is witness to the manner in which David's agony is caught up into the Passion story and the exaltation of the Messiah (Acts 4.25–28).

David, when the reality of Absalom's revolt and the horror of it broke with force upon his mind, turned naturally to the wider and the national implications of the perilous situation. Perhaps it is more likely to imagine his making swift and effective arrangements, first to meet the tactical situation, and then, on the march or at Mahanaim, turning to the strategic situation.

David had devoted much activity, recorded and unrecorded. to the establishment of the safety of the borders. From then till today, the frontiers of Israel were intricate, beleaguered, and difficult to defend. In pacifying the borderlands the king had made many enemies. Consider Ammon, and the hostilities between that border-tribe and Israel. This was one only of those who surrounded a damaged realm with menace.

Damaged, the realm certainly was. Swift messengers would convey the news to Damascus, and the rest of the enemy capitals, that rebellion was afoot. Absalom was base enough to solicit aid. By what devices David secured the peace, which, in the end, gave him time to defeat the rebellion without invasion from abroad, is not recorded in the story, but may be guessed from the psalm.

Two matters are certain. One is that the situation was dangerous in the extreme. The nations were conspiring and the peoples plotting. That the plotting was 'in vain' (1, RSV), at this point, was only a reality in David's new-born faith. The second matter is that somehow David's quick diplomacy kept the foreigners quiet. His line of retreat lay in the direction of the eastern frontier. This was, to be sure, a guerrilla tactic. David fell back on the friendly wilderness. He also moved in the direction of the foe.

There is a hint here for times of trouble. Put on God's armour, move in the direction of the available resources. Move also towards, not away from, the foe. Be firm. Probably such courageous language as that of vs. 10–12 daunted the enemy, and won the battle before it really began.


## 30 : Dawn

### Psalm 3; 2 Timothy 2.1–13

A map should at this point be consulted if the perils of the royal fugitive, and his reactions to them, are to be understood. His retreat had as its goal the ancient town of Mahanaim, to the north-east and far across the Jordan Valley. The direct route would be down the Jericho road, across the river there, and then north to the desired point. David would surely avoid the open road, and strike north-east in as direct a route as possible. It was a rough march from the highlands of Jerusalem to the deep Jordan Rift far below sea-level, a wilderness journey, dropping 4,000 feet, and then up the Jabbok gorge to the plateau.

Psa. 3 is a morning prayer, probably uttered on the first dawn of the retreat. The word 'many' appears three times in the Hebrew of vs. 1 to 6, four times if we include the verb of similar root in v. 6 'God, how *many* are those who oppress me, *many* are in revolt against me, *many* are saying of my soul: "No help for him in God." ' Snatching an image from the shield under which he has lain all night, David picks up the speech of the old promise to Abraham (Gen. 15.1). Shimei's words were still echoing in his mind. The memory of old sin which they had roused was gnawing. It was with an effort of faith that David called God 'his glory'. Earthly glory was gone. His reputation was in ruins. It was a challenge to courage and to faith to believe that God had forgiven, had restored and lifted the fallen. And yet that is what the sinner who has truly repented is called upon to do. We must forgive ourselves for those sins which God has forgiven us. To grovel in them is morbid.

With the sixth verse we see confidence flowing back. The

49

first mood, when the harassed man woke under the paling stars, had been to think of all the land raised in revolt against him. Prayer, however, was healing his hurt. Faith was returning. Around him on the hillside faithful men were also stirring. And Absalom had not attacked, though scarce a score of miles lay behind and between them. Nor was there any indication of pursuit. And so, with the next verse, faith lays hold of the reality yet to be. It was a fact that, by not winning with a swift decisive stroke that day, as Ahithophel had advised, Absalom had lost the war. But only faith could see it thus at the moment. Faith did.

## 31 : Evening

### Psalms 4 and 7

There is a very clear link between Psa. **4** and its predecessor. The writer had been haunted by his own words, as the little band of refugees struggled all day down the rough slopes towards the Jordan valley. 'My glory' ('honour', RSV, translates the same Hebrew word), 'there are many who say', 'In peace I will both lie down and sleep', are obvious echoes. Add the fact that this is an evening prayer. Twelve hours lie between the two psalms.

It is also a prayer of thankfulness. The worst has not happened. The rebel prince had again missed the opportunity for pursuit. He was again the victim of his own shallow and volatile personality, enjoying the plaudits of Jerusalem, riding the tide of transient popularity, defiling the palace . . .

The future lay in the hands of the dusty train of fugitives, every hour a rough mile or two nearer to safety in the wild country their leader knew so well. And hour by hour, to David's jubilant relief, the scouts came in to report no sign of pursuit.

The key sentence in the opening verse runs: 'In narrow places you have made space for me.' Moffatt turns it well: 'O **God, my** champion . . . When I was hemmed in, thou hast freed me often.' David was looking for space. He had often known such escape from Saul's cordon and desert siege. The city had filled him with claustrophobia. He was himself now that he was out of it.

Life feels like that at times. Circumstances hem us in, and

50

fill us with that 'quiet desperation' which Thoreau regarded as the commonest mood of man. There are times when troubles throng around, and there is no clear horizon. At such times there is one course only possible—move straight along the path which faith and deepest instinct have dictated as right, not doubting in the dark what God has shown to be our duty in the light. Men had turned David's royal glory into shame (2), as they turn God's glory into shame, defiling all beauty, spoiling with soiled hands all lovely and fragile things, corrupting the glory of music, speech, the landscape, love . . . all else; 'because,' as Chesterton said, 'it is only Christian men keep even heathen things.' Why? Because as the same verse (2) says, 'they seek after sham ('lies', RSV). 'You men,' the Jerusalem Bible puts it, 'why shut your hearts so long, loving delusions, chasing after lies?'

## 32 : Night

### Psalms 4 and 8

We must spend some more time on Psa. 4. This group of psalms, all of which appear to have been born of the Absalom rebellion, gives deep insights into David's character and his spiritual experience. Psa. 4 is clearly an evening prayer (8). The party is well down the rough hillsides which lead to the Jordan and safety. The sun has disappeared behind the western ridge where Jerusalem stands. The mountains of Moab have turned purple and dark. Evening moves to night.

In the last study we followed David to v. 3. He now touches with precision and insight on the reason for man's tinkering and spoiling of God's good. We shall follow here the AV(KJV). 'Stand in awe, and sin not', is the correct translation. The word is rendered 'tremble' in Psa. 99.1. In a word, the psalmist has reached a deep conclusion: 'Bow in reverential wonder before the Almighty, and the spirit of rebellion and human pride will wither.' The wilderness is teaching its old, clear lessons to its wandering son, who had been driven home again.

It is true that the Christian does not 'tremble' before God (see 1 John 2.28 in Phillips' translation). 'Bold I approach the eternal throne,' runs Wesley's hymn (Heb. 10.19–24). At the same time a proper appreciation of the Eternal God inspires awe (Psa. **8**). David saw that in the deadening atmosphere of the city he had lost something of his reverence for the One who had seemed so near, so great, so wondrous under the turning constellation of the desert night. Verse 4 is the central thought of the whole psalm. Such is the theme, it concludes, for night-time meditation. And that is why Psa. **8** is prescribed as a reading. 'Commune with your own hearts . . . and be silent.' Prayer needs no special language. 'Be silent' . . . In such surrender it is possible to listen, too.

Psa. **4**.5 then calls for simple faith. David had already named 'a humble and a contrite heart'—'a broken spirit; a broken and contrite heart' (**51**.17 RSV), as God's requirements. He makes such sacrifice in the very act of speech. He then can face the murmuring of the weary band. He had heard the soldiers' grumble during the weary day (6). But he can now pull his cloak around him, and sleep in confidence, sure that He who has led so far will, on the morrow, lead on.

## 33 : Morning Again

### Psalms 5 and 11

Verse 3 shows Psa. **5** to be a morning prayer, and adds force to the contention that these early psalms are a series consequent on the third. It is the second morning of the retreat, and the river, with its surrounding jungle, was at no great distance. There was still harsh journeying, but up the Jabbok gorge and the pasture-lands beyond lay safety.

Verse 3 speaks twice of the morning, and v. 12 resumes the image of the shield. All these facts show that an ordered sequence of thought and experience runs through the words. But David is calmer now, and thinks of prayer in quieter fashion. Moffatt renders the opening clauses: '. . . listen to my words, and hear the murmur of my soul . . . give ear to my appeal.' There are 'sighs too deep for words' (Rom. **8**.26, RSV) which are none the less true prayer, for prayer is 'the heart's sincere desire, uttered or unexpressed.' Quiet prayer, coherent prayer, incoherent longing, and agonized petition, are all included here. David felt them all, as, from the lower slopes of the bare Judean hills, he looked across the green broad ribbon of the Jordan plain and the tortuous river to the blue and mauve transjordanian ranges.

This is a carefully ordered prayer, as if the writer had slightly more time for composition. Four verses (4–7) speak of the confession with which true prayer must begin. David prepares his soul for the Royal Presence, and thinks of folly, falsehood, and harm to others—perhaps the sins which, at that moment of contrite review, lay most heavily upon his conscience. Nothing so distorts prayer as insincerity, posing or falsehood of any sort. 'Lying,' said the old French essayist Montaigue, 'is a hateful and accursed thing. We should pursue it with fire and sword.' 'Sin,' said Oliver Wendell Holmes, 'has many tools, but a lie is the handle which fits them all.' Remembering Bathsheba and Uriah, David knew this truth full well. He faced it and purged the memory away. His mind was back again at the opening verses of the psalm of the previous morning, and his humble acceptance of the foul words of Shimei.

Passing from meditation to petition David begs for safety and guidance (8). He begged for a straight path, literally, for there was rough land and doubtful loyalty ahead, and spiritually, for he needed desperately the counsel God alone could give. Verses 9 and 10 are a sudden outburst, the 'cry' of v. 2. Caught in a burst of agony, David cries out in a fashion a New Testament Christian can hardly follow, but rapidly calms into the final two verses. The shield is God's peace and it comes to submission. 'Peace,' said Fénélon, 'does not dwell in outward things but in the soul. We may preserve it in the midst of bitterest pain, if our will remains firm and submissive. Peace in this life springs from acquiescence, not in exemption from suffering.' The king of Israel was learning this old lesson anew.

## 34 : Valley of Shadow

### Psalms 6 and 10

In the morning prayer of Psa. 5, David fought his way through to peace of mind, and quiet confidence in God. Now comes Psa. 6, a prayer, if our guess be true, of that same day's night. It is a sombre psalm, and the physical exhaustion of the day which preceded it must be taken into account if the mood of gloom and groping which fills the psalm is to be understood. Perils from the enemy had receded, but it must be remembered that David and his followers were short of food and water, and had now struggled through shockingly difficult terrain for three days. The narrow flood plain of the Zor, through which the Jordan cuts its serpentine path, was most difficult to break through. The fugitives must have found it peculiarly exhausting, and sheer weariness can daunt the soul, and, in the sensitive, precipitate a mood of pessimism. We should understand this natural reaction.

Then, if it is correctly assumed that the line of march was north-east to the point where the Jabbok joins the Jordan, another grim journey awaited. The route would run up the sinister Jabbok gorge, scene of Jacob's old wrestling, to the uplands and the hoped-for safety of Mahanaim. It was a long haul up the bed of the stream. The cliffs press in and overwhelm the traveller. From the night's sojourn there, and the depressing landscape, David was to draw the imagery of the Valley of the Shadow of Death, a word-picture which he wove into the best known of all his psalms. But that was not until next day.

Anxiety, too, marched with him, for no one, at this stage could tell whether they might find disaffection or loyalty at Mahanaim. But it was David's way to put all he felt and feared into prayer. Hence the opening words of Psa. **6**, short sharp cries for help. God does not mistake the voice of fear for the voice of impiety. It is all very well for preachers to comment with prim disapproval on 'the sin of anxiety'. God does not regard fear, depression, deep worry or solicitude as sin, provided they are brought in frankness to His feet and placed in His creative hands.

## Themes for study and discussion on Studies 29–34

1. 'Great David's greater Son' in Psa. 2.
2. How faith returns after failure.
3. The place of awe in true religion.
4. The need to pray when the day is in prospect and when it is in retrospect.
5. 'Trouble produces better poems than ease.'

# MAN AND SIN

## Fallen: The New Testament

### 35: The Slavery of Sin

#### John 8.30–47

The key to this passage is to be found in v. 32. Jesus there speaks about the emancipation which results from a knowledge of the truth. The Jews retort that as Abraham's descendants they have never experienced bondage. Clearly they have failed to grasp what Jesus meant.

In v. 34 He explains what kind of slavery He had in mind. In 'one of the most remarkable sayings ever uttered by our Lord' (W. Hendriksen) the announcement is made that universal sin implies universal slavery. All who commit sin are slaves to it and since all sin, all are slaves. Jesus does not spell out the details of this proposition, but its logic is not lost on His hearers. The proud distinction of Jews from Gentiles is obliterated, since basically all men are equal in the sight of God—equal in sin (cf. Rom. 6.16; 2 Pet. 2.19). Even the pagan philosophers agreed. Seneca declared that no bondage is more severe than that of the passions, and Plato wrote that liberty is the name of virtue and slavery the name of vice. Jesus then goes on to make a rather different application of the slave metaphor, indicating, however, that in every sense the truest freedom is to be found in Himself (35 f.).

A discussion then follows as to the ancestry of the Jews (39–47). Our Lord's refusal to recognize them as children of Abraham or of God may be applied to any who claim relationship to God by reason of national, family or ecclesiastical connections. Evidence of kinship is shown in resemblance.

The devil is described as a killer (cf. 1 John 3.15) and a liar (44). It was he who first introduced sin to man and death through sin (Rom. 5.12). It was by misrepresentation that he tempted Eve (Gen. 3.4), and he is still the one who deceives the world (Rev. **12**.9). By nature every man is not only a slave of the devil but is his child and takes after his father, Only by grace can he become a child of God as he trusts in Christ who is the Truth (John **14**.6),

## 36 : Suffering and Sin

### John 9

Our Lord's encounter with a man afflicted by congenital blindness raised the issue of the relationship between suffering and sin. 'The question is as old as humanity' (J. H. Bernard). The first answer the disciples suggested was not a feasible solution. Since this man had been blind from birth only some far-fetched hypothesis of pre-existence could lend it support.

The second suggestion reflected the prevailing view in Judaism. The reply of Jesus, however, rejected both these theories. No doubt all suffering is in some way the result of sin, but that is only half the story, and this was not a case where a specific sin had incurred a specific penalty. A backward look traces the connection not indeed between sins and sins but between sin and sin, since all are born in sin (34). A forward look, however, discerns the providential purpose of God which utilizes such suffering to reveal His power.

Such questions are still asked. Blindness is not the only congenital condition which afflicts human beings. The disciples were puzzled but perhaps detached questioners. Such questions gain an added and often an anguished dimension when they are asked from within the family of the afflicted. Where mere human sympathy and wisdom are so inadequate, the words of Him who plumbed the depths of human sorrow and suffering at Calvary have a power to comfort which is all their own, as so many distressed yet trusting believers have discovered.

More serious than the physical blindness recorded here is the spiritual blindness of the Pharisees, because they are altogether unconscious of it (40 f.). Christ not only came that the blind might see, but also that those who claim to see might become blind (Mark **4**.12). The very fact that the Pharisees imagine they are equipped with spiritual vision aggravates their guilt. Archbishop Temple warned against trying to keep our eyes half open and to live by half the light, 'That kind of sight holds us to our sin and our sin to us.'

*A thought : What helps so much here is not only what is said but who it is that says it.*

## 37 : The Curse of Adam

### Romans 5.12–21

This is the most extensive New Testament commentary on the fall. The implications of Adam's sin are drawn out, and we are shown how the work of Christ as the last Adam reversed that of the first.

'All men sinned' (12) does not simply mean that at some time or other everyone has been guilty of transgression. The context makes it clear that what the apostle intends to affirm is the more fundamental fact that all sinned representatively when Adam sinned. Mankind is regarded as an organic unity. It is a single body under a single head. Adam is the head of the old aeon of death as Christ is the head of the new aeon of life. The sinful fate of humanity was representatively and historically determined in Adam in the same way that the road to salvation was opened up representatively and historically in Christ. In each case it was through 'one man' (12, 15–18), as representing all. The similarities and contrasts are worked out in a fivefold series (15–19).

'Death through sin' (12) is another recurring theme in this passage (14 f., 17, 21). The intrusion of death—and the reference here is to physical as well as to eternal death—is a consequence of the fall. Exile from Eden involved exclusion from the tree of life (Gen. 3.24). Paul tells us that death spread to all men' (12)—it made its way to each member of the human race and gained the mastery over them. All this was 'because all men sinned in Adam' (12). Recent translations support this traditional interpretation of *eph ho* as 'because' in preference to 'under these conditions' or 'in so far as'.

The relationship of sin to the law is considered in v. 13 and taken up again in vs. 20 f. Like sin and death, law too came in' (20). Its effect was to multiply sin. Sin, of course, was present in the world long before the law as such was introduced, but it could not be charged up. When the law was formulated, it intensified and in some instances even provoked transgression. The very prohibition sometimes adds an attraction to sin for the rebellious heart. Law, then, only aggravated the fall. But for 'grace abounding' man could never have recovered.

## Questions and themes for study and discussion on Studies 35–37

1. It has been said that man is only really free when nothing that can harm him has any power over him. Do you agree?

2. How can the biblical doctrine of providence be employed in seeking to help those perplexed by problems of human suffering and affliction?

3. Does Paul's teaching give us any idea as to *how* Adam's descendants become involved in his fall and its results?

# CHARACTER STUDIES

## 38 : Barzillai

### 2 Samuel 17.27-29; John 6.67-71; Matthew 16.13-20

David's instinct was sound. It was safe to retire to the old sources of his help and loyalty among the shepherd-folk of the hills. All through the Bible runs a thread to be traced from Abraham abiding in the hills when Lot chose the plain, on to the shepherd-men of Bethlehem round whom God's glory shone. Here was the old core of the land's worth and faithfulness, abiding sure when corruption ate up the souls of men in the cities, and religion withered in urban corruption.

Little is said in the record of the bitter march which we have tried to trace behind the utterances of a series of psalms. And one psalm remains, the most famous of all. But before we turn to its well-known words we shall look at the man who provided the glad occasion, Barzillai, the sheep-rancher of Mahanaim and Gilead.

When David's little band struggled up out of the Jabbok gorge and the Jordan jungle, some anxieties fell to rest. Shobi (27) was the son of Hanun, who so scurrilously insulted David's envoys and occasioned the Ammon war (2 Sam. **10**). David had set him on Hanun's throne and his loyalty held. Machir was a local sheik. He had been a supporter of Saul and had given political asylum to Mephibosheth. David's generous treatment of Jonathan's lame son had won his allegiance. The perilous border-lands were not aflame.

The third benefactor was a rich man of Gilead, and the subsequent story singles him out as leader in this demonstration of loyalty. He was an old man, in fact eighty years old, 'a great and good man,' said Josephus, 'who made plentiful provision at Mahanaim.' It was loyalty which refreshed David more than all the provender set before him. Loyalty which awaits no demonstration of advantage, but stakes its all in a doubtful day, is precious to the soul. And such a man was Barzillai, like Milton's Abdiel:

59

> *Among the faithless, faithful only he,*
> *Among innumerable false, unmoved,*
> *Unshaken, unseduced, unterrified,*
> *His loyalty he kept, his love, his zeal.*

The Lord seeks such men. And in days of stress He sometimes refreshes the harassed soul of His hard-pressed servants by the revelation of such presences. 'A bold spirit in a loyal breast' is a prime offering to Him and to those we love. Granted that reinforcement, a man can often face the world which might otherwise destroy him.

## 39 : Royal Guest

### Psalm 23; John 10.1–18

Mahanaim, as we have seen, brought no betrayal, only friendship, and the glorious hospitality of the shepherd, Barzillai. It was delightful country, after the horrors of the Jordan jungle and the Jabbok ravine. Fears were laid to rest, and prayer, which at times had slipped into the language of desperation, was obviously answered.

Perhaps it was when the sun was sloping towards the far blue horizon where Jerusalem was, and rebel Absalom, that the feast was spread 'in the presence of David's enemies'. And when the feast was over, then it was perhaps that the royal guest rose to his feet to say thanks to his shepherd host. How better could he express his gratitude than to liken the gracious care of the great ranch-owner, and the host of that same afternoon, to God Himself, who had so obviously guided, so clearly spread the table of His grace? This is perhaps what the psalmist guest did. Was this the inspiration of the Shepherd Psalm?

The simplicity of the words is the mark and sign of David's return to the faith of his boyhood. Here is the high peak of his restoration. Here he stands at his best, brought back to the faith and purity which had once made him the 'man after God's own heart'. We should observe him well, for the years were soon to take their grim toll, and the royal psalmist was to become the sad wreck which we see in the final chapters of his life.

Read this psalm several times. No translation should tamper with the fragile cadences of the AV (KJV). It is correctly rendered there, and whoever translated it was a master of English, and a man of sensitive feeling for language. The shepherd image should be followed through Scripture. It occurs five times in Psa. **74** to **80**. It runs from Moses to Christ. The Eastern shepherd went before, with crook to restrain and cudgel to defend. He was there along the lighted path, and in the dark shades of the valley. And beyond the valley lies the 'house of the Lord', where the redeemed shall live for ever. The psalm thus concludes with words not uncommon in the Old Testament, which almost break through to that confidence in another life which was not to become clear till Christ defeated death (2 Tim. **1**.10). Read the psalm yet again and understand the beauty of the writer's mind.

## 40 : 'Absalom, my Son'

### 2 Samuel 18.1–19.8

The rebellion was over. Absalom's attempt to destroy David with conventional forces in a conventional attack failed, as it was bound to do, when David fell back on the tactics of guerrilla war. Conscious of David's pathological weakness for his rebel son, the commanders had persuaded the king to remain behind in the town. The battle in the Gilead oak woods closed with Absalom's ludicrous death, caught by the hair in a tree. Joab was determined, with his rough notions of justice, that the prince should not survive his deluded followers, who lay in their thousands on the scrub-covered hillsides.

Joab defied his royal master, as he consistently did. He had held an ascendancy over David since the king made him an accomplice in Uriah's murder. And indeed, at this moment, Joab knew what was better for the country than his uncle did. Yearning and sorrow over a perverted young criminal had no doubt their pathos, but showed small concern for the devoted loyalists who had fought and fallen on that same day. No psalm, no salutary word, flowed from that last grief. It was not committed to God. It was an incongruity which Joab rightly rebuked, a shameful selfishness.

The psalms of the great rebellion were, in fact, over. They were in the last brilliant uprising of David's devotion and his song. They were the rich fruit of his last suffering. David had nothing more to give. In a later chapter (22) the chronicler records a song of deliverance, but the words are those of Psa. 18, written long years before.

Perhaps Absalom killed his father. The last flame of his energy and his poetic genius flared high during the retreat, but left only ashes behind. The shock of Absalom's death was deadly. Perhaps, and the word must be used again as we grope for truth behind the too brief record, perhaps David had hoped in his folly that Absalom would succeed him. His judgement was certainly corrupt and weak in these sad closing days. To put Amasa in Joab's place (19.13) was an act of crass folly, and certain to result in misery. David could not have been much over sixty years of age, but the rest of his life, perhaps ten years, is full of the marks of senility. It is sad to see the blight that had fallen on his life run its sad course.

## 41 : David Comes Home

### 2 Samuel 19.15–30, 41–43; 20.1–3

Here was a sorry homecoming. The returning exiles crossed the Jordan by an easier ford than that which they had used along the jungle route. Shimei, the harsh-tongued critic of the retreat, was there on the river bank to grovel before the man whom he had insulted, and won a generous pardon, later treacherously repudiated. Mephibosheth also appeared, and convinced the king that Ziba, his servant, had played him false, and in the same act had as basely deceived David He received less than justice. Ziba was allowed to retain half of the reward of his crime (29). The suspicion lurks that David was saving face after his deception by Ziba, and was not ready to admit his fault and put right a hasty decision which had gravely wronged a son of Jonathan.

The whole impression he gives at this time is that of a physically and mentally exhausted man, making hasty decisions often patently unwise. He was probably in no state to deal basically with the rift between his own men of Judah and the rest of the land. The appointment of Amasa to the high command was, perhaps, a fumbling attempt at conciliation, but it was without success, and nothing appears to have been done to damp the too obvious enthusiasm of the men of David's own tribe.

It was Judah which had facilitated David's crossing of the Jordan, and very rapidly an open breach appeared (**19**.41–43). David's old gifts of leadership seem to have gone. Perhaps Joab knew how to give the impression that the king was old, the king was a figurehead, the king had lost his dash and initiative. The story is a sad one, and Israel's response rapidly deteriorated into open revolt.

Back in Jerusalem David sequestered the harem girls who had been the victims of Absalom, by no fault other than David's own. The establishment was shameful for one as enlightened as David, as we have already remarked, set a base example for Solomon, and led to a life of unhappiness for ten helpless women. They received no protection from the king when he evacuated Jerusalem. They had small consideration now. It is so difficult to isolate vice. With shocking exactitude every breach of the moral law exacts its sanctions.

## 42 : Joab the Murderous

### 2 Samuel 19.9–14; 20.4–13

Joab was a rough and powerful man. He knew how to bide his time. David appointed Amasa, Absalom's commander, to lead his army, either to convince the rebel soldiers that no reprisals awaited them, or to punish Joab for the death of the infamous Absalom. Whatever the motive, it was a lamentable piece of foolishness. Whatever comfort it might have brought to the survivors of Absalom's unfortunate host, what sort of spirit was such an act likely to arouse in the minds of those who had followed David in an evil day, and suffered with him?

Joab, furthermore, was the sort of leader that simple fighting men admire, brave, determined and downright. Joab did not lose his confidence. Sheba led his brief revolt. The land was again in an uproar, and Amasa was sent out with a royal mandate to mobilize a task force in three days. It proved impossible, and indeed Amasa's record as a soldier was not one which suggested notable competence in such matters. Amasa's levy failed to appear.

Impatiently the king sent Abishai after Sheba, and with Abishai went Joab, who seems to have retained control of David's two bands of crack mercenary troops (**20**.7, cf. **15**.18). Joab, when aroused, was capable of any crime, and he had long brooded over his supersession by Amasa. His brother Abishai, under whom at this moment he was nominally serving, had been his partner in an earlier assassination (**3**.27–30), and could do little to restrain Joab in an exactly similar set of circumstances. David had used him to murder Uriah. It was a situation David might have foreseen. He was helpless.

Joab now took command, with or without Abishai's compliance. The pursuit of Sheba continued, and in the far north of the land the rebel was brought to bay. He was a Benjaminite, probably of the house of Saul, and in his rebellion was canalized the jealousy against Judah, which Judah had done nothing to allay (**19**.15). It was a portent of what was to be after Solomon's oppressive reign. The tribal divisions, which had wrecked the land in the days of the judges, were not healed.

So Joab handed over command of the household troops on which he had cynically and bloodily ridden to renewed power, and resumed control of the armies of Israel in David's despite.

## 43 : Chimham

### 2 Samuel 19.31–40; 1 Kings 2.7; Jeremiah 41.17; Luke 2.8–16

With gracious courtesy old Barzillai accompanied his king to the limits of his native trans-Jordan territory. With fine common sense he refused honours which no longer attracted him. With admirable unselfishness he sought not to make his aged presence a burden to others (35). With quiet dignity he sought the king's favour for his son Chimham.

It would appear from the brief reference in 1 Kings, that

David gave the son of Barzillai the task for which he was fitted—the care of the sheep on the ancestral pasturelands of Jesse's family at Bethlehem. Like his father, Chimham knew what he could do, what would give him joy and fulfilment, and sought to do it. A portion of the estate seems to have passed to his possession.

At the risk of building too large a structure on slender foundations, shall we speculate a little further? Chimham brought two traditions from his father's home, shepherding and hospitality. Did he make the Bethlehem estate a centre for shepherds, and a refuge for the good men of the land? Did the hostelry which Chimham established remain in the family, after the stable fashion of the east, and become the 'geruth', or caravanserai, of the Jeremiah passage, where Johanan found shelter along with the little band of refugees after Nebuchadnezzar had destroyed Jerusalem?

That was four centuries later. Dare we move on six centuries more and ask why the shepherds thought immediately of Bethlehem when they heard of the Nativity? Was the inn at Bethlehem the same establishment, and was the innkeeper's name Chimham? Hospitality on that notable occasion had not failed as lamentably as some believe. 'Kataluma' (Luke 2.7) should not, in fact, be translated 'inn'. It means 'guest-chamber' and on the night of the census would be occupied by those of David's line who arrived first, Hillel and Simeon, perhaps, the leading Pharisees. Mary was given the next best accommodation, with no slight or rejection implied in it, probably a cavern, as tradition states, with a raised platform where visitors could watch over their beasts and baggage. So the old tradition of hospitality did not falter. A thread runs from Barzillai's banquet to the Holy Family, if we speculate aright, and to the Lord Himself. It matters much what traditions we establish in our families. They can be amazingly persistent.

### Questions and themes for study and discussion on Studies 38–43

1. What is the test of true loyalty?

2. In Psa. 23.1 we usually stress the possessive pronoun. Where is the emphasis likely to have fallen in David's mind?

3. Ending well.

4. The wisdom of delaying important decisions, where possible, until rest of body and mind aids clear-sightedness.

5. The place of the shepherd and of pastoral imagery in the spiritual message of the Bible.

# MAN AND SIN

## A Guilty Rebel: Recognized in the Old Testament

### 44 : Unconscious Offences

#### Leviticus 5

This chapter forms part of the Manual of Sacrifice (**1**.3–**7**.38) which from **4**.1 to **6**.7 gives instructions to the people about offerings for sin. 'We are dealing with sacrificial procedure having expiatory effects' (M.Noth). A special type of trespass is considered in **5**.1–13, which is an appendix to ch. **4**. It has to do with unconscious offences in which a man only realizes later that he has infringed the law. Even such lapses, however trivial they may seem, are regarded as sinful.

In the first case (1), someone fails to come forward and give evidence, even after there has been a public appeal. Of course, there may be a deliberate refusal to testify, but in the context a misunderstanding of the summons or a defective sense of duty is implied. The second is a case of cultic uncleanness through accidental contact either with an animal or a man (2 f.). The taboos are tabulated in chs. **12–15** and the penalty of excommunication prescribed (Num. **19**.13, 20). If the purification has been omitted through ignorance, however, guilt can be covered by the sin offering. The third case is that of a rashly sworn vow (whether good or bad) which a man forgets he has made or does not realize is culpable (4). It is not clear whether the offering actually procures his release from the oath.

All these offences require confession of sin before the entire community (5 f.) and the presentation of the sin offering 'as his penalty for the sin that he has committed' (NEB). To translate as 'guilt offering' (AV, RV, RSV) is misleading since *asam* is here used non-technically (as also in v. 7).

Verses 14–19 deal with the guilt offering as such, although N.H. Snaith prefers to call it a compensation offering. The Jerusalem Bible has 'reparation'. The word has to do with

67

liability for repayment. Each of these cases involves fraud. 'The holy things of the Lord' (15) include the gifts and tithes which were the perquisites of the priests. If these were not up to standard, or actually withheld, and this was shown to be intentional, the death penalty could be imposed (Num. **15**.31). But if it was an unwitting offence, restitution had to be made in full plus a twenty per cent fine. In the case of a completely unknown fault the compensation offering was required but not the compensation payment.

Man is regarded as responsible to God even when he sins in ignorance. Otherwise it would pay not to know. In fact, the passage teaches us that no transgression of the Law of God is to be viewed as of little account. Nothing which caused suffering to Christ (whose sacrifice is the anti-type of all the Levitical offerings) can be treated as trivial by His redeemed.


## 45 : Not One Good

### Psalm 14

The psalm opens with a lament about the depravity of the wicked, cast, as Weiser explains, in the form of a prophet's forceful denunciation (1 ff.). The *nabal* is not merely a fool, but a much more aggressive character who is militant in his denial of God (1). Behind the devastating corruption that runs through the whole of society lies the refusal to recognize the existence of the moral claims of a holy God.

In a picture full of pathos, the Lord Himself is described as gazing down from heaven on all mankind to discover if any have enough sense to seek Him out. The conclusion of v. 3. is comprehensive. All without exception have proved disloyal ('turned aside' is used of going after other gods; cf. Exod. **32**.8; Judg. **2**.17). and are 'rotten to the core' (NEB). Not even one can be found who is not tainted by sin. It is this verse that Paul quotes in Rom. **3**.10.

Even pagan writers have conceded the universal inclination of man to evil. Horace declared that no one is born without faults and that even if nature is driven away with a pitchfork it continually returns. The Jewish rabbis had to admit that even the most pious of the pious were nevertheless guilty in at least one direction. The trouble with modern man is that, although recognizing the same fact after a fashion, he tries to turn the edge of it by appeals to the 'animal nature' resulting from evolution or by some other natural factor. Sin is the last realm in which we want 'to call a spade a spade'.

The sins which spring from a rejection of God are indicated throughout the psalm. They include corruption (1), alienation (2), infidelity (3), cruelty (4), prayerlessness (4), and derision (6). These are only samples, for in fact 'every crime in the book' stems from the same source. That is why the Bible interprets sin as unbelief. It is more than breaking rules. It is a breach of fellowship between man and God. It is a fractured relationship. Those who in the spurious wisdom of their own conceit decide that there is no God cannot even begin to please Him. That is why atheism is the ultimate folly. It is a repudiation of God's sovereignty.


# 46 : The Lessons of History

## Psalm 78.1–31

Here we are invited to look into what Delitzsch called 'the warning mirror of history', in order to learn the lessons of the past. The psalmist conducts us through the archives of Israel from Moses to David. His purpose is not so much to focus our attention on antiquity as to show the relevance of previous events for our current situation. The philosopher Benedetto Croce has said that all history is contemporary in the sense that it has contributed to what is happening now and is thus part of the living present. This is especially true of redemption history.

In vs. 1–8 the psalmist indicates that he has a *maskil* (parable) to deliver (2). He will 'expound the riddle of things past' (NEB). Before he turns to God's miracle of deliverance at the Red Sea (12–13), he voices a complaint against the Ephraimites because of their defection (9 ff.). They are singled out from the rest of the tribes as being exceptionally reprehensible. They committed the unpardonable sin, militarily speaking: they deserted in the middle of a battle. An actual incident is not identified: it may have been a general reluctance to implement the conquest of Canaan.

We get some hints as to why they cracked under pressure. They shared the general deterioration of a spineless age. Their hearts were not fixed on God (8). There was a failure in orientation. Moreover, they proved unfaithful to the covenant which undergirded the whole relationship between Yahweh and His people (10a). They even set aside the demands of the law, refusing to walk along the path it laid down (10b). Worse still, they forgot what God had done (11). The recollection of His protecting mercy, which should have spurred them on to further exploits, had faded from their minds. This is how the devil still tempts us to quit the fight. We must be aware of his methods.

The overall failure of the Israelites themselves is pinpointed in v. 22. They did not fully trust in God nor did they really believe in His ability to rescue them (cf. Num. **14**.11). They did not realize that the exodus from Egypt was a sign of God's continuing help. They still dubiously enquired, 'Can God?' (19 f.). Doubt is a frequent ingredient of sin. Only when we are convinced that God can shall we gain the victory.


## 47 : A Portrait of the Heart

### Psalm 78.32–66

Persistence in sin (32), despite the marvels of God's intervening grace, deserves and receives His disciplinary chastisement (33). The reference may be to the judgement of death threatened on those of twenty years old and upwards after the departure from Egypt (Num. **14**.12, 28 ff.). The effect of this punitive measure was to jolt God's children out of their spiritual complacency (34). 'When he struck them, they began to seek him' (NEB).

But in vs. 36 f. we find that their repentance was unreal. They went through the appropriate motions and uttered the ritual incantations (36), but they still remained faithless at heart (37). They pretended to be contrite for fear of what might be visited upon them and not because they had a genuine love of righteousness. Yet even in the face of such dissembling, God restrained His wrath in compassion and

70

still continued to forgive (38). The long-suffering of God is movingly depicted.

The reason for His forbearance is disclosed in v. 39. It is that, as Psa. **103**.14 expresses it, 'he knows our frame; he remembers that we are dust.' He took into consideration the moral helplessness of man. The reference to the flesh implies ethical impotence as well as the transitoriness of mortal life (cf. Gen. **6**.3; **8**.21). The repeated intransigence of the Israelites is contrasted with God's everlasting mercy in vs. 40–55. The section from v. 56 to v. 72 speaks of renewed rebellion, in particular through idolatrous entanglement (58). The sinful condition of God's people is graphically summarized in v. 57. They were like a bow with a warp (Jerusalem Bible) which cannot be used by the archer (Hos. **7**.16). It lets the arrow fly off at a tangent. Even when the Israelites attempted to return to God, they deviated from Him and thus disappointed His expectations. No wonder their ingrained recalcitrance 'provoked most justly' His 'wrath and indignation'.

Such an historical psalm makes us aware of the fact that church history contains examples of similar sins, translated from national into ecclesiastical terms. And what of the individual? Do we not all have times of rebellion to confess? Is the Christian's penitence as deep as it should be? Where would *I* be without the long-suffering of God? And yet how unthinkable that I should ever presume on it in the face of Calvary!

## Questions and themes for study and discussion on Studies 44–47

1. To what extent do the Levitical regulations concerning unconscious offences bear on the Christian conception of sin?

2. Compare Psa. **14** with Psa. **53**. Can you suggest any *spiritual* reason why we should have been given two psalms that are almost identical?

3. Compare Psa. **78** with Acts **7**. What lesson do they teach in common? Do any other psalms deal with Israel's history as the story of her faithlessness and rebellion?

# CHARACTER STUDIES

## 48 : David and the Gibeonites

### 2 Samuel 21

This is a difficult chapter, and might be omitted were it not part of the purpose before us to see the character of David in its entirety. Briefly, the chapter tells of the cruel and bloody avenging of old wrongs upon the innocent, the ghastly murder of Saul's decendants, and an exhibition of cruelty relieved only by the heroism and reverence of Rizpah, whose act seems to have touched David to pity.

The difficulty of the narrative lies in v. 14, where it appears to be stated that God, after the fashion of some pagan deity, a Moloch or some offended demon from the Greek pantheon, was appeased by human sacrifice. It has been clearly enough laid down in Scripture, from Abraham on through the Law, that Yahweh countenanced no human sacrifice. His law cannot have been varied on this occasion. Verse 14 need imply no more than that, after these panic-stricken deeds of blood, the pleas of a broken people were heard, and the famine passed. Certainly no sanguinary sacrifice released God's hand.

In point of fact, Israel and the eastern lands of the Mediterranean were passing through a century of climatological crises, the course of which can be traced in the archaeology of the middle Mediterranean and the Aegean world. God's purposes are intertwined with history, and there was a wrong to Gibeon which demanded righting. David was called to do this, and the urge was of God. The alien tribe was perhaps overlooked in the famine-relief operations which must have been in train, and justice could have been done here.

Where David was at fault was in listening to the voice of savagery. The Gibeonites were aliens outside the old tradition, and the opportunity before David was to enlighten them in the ways of mercy which he knew well enough. Instead he listened to their barbarism. Again we seem to see a damaged spirit. We view the aged David correctly when we see a man worn by the toils of an arduous life, surrounded by lesser and by vicious men, a man of deep spiritual insight struggling with the drag and tug of an age which did not understand his higher aspirations, and now, at last, with capacities failing, and burdens of his own making lying heavily on his heart, succumbing to pride, cruelty and lamentable error.

## 49 : David's Memories

### 2 Samuel 22

The closing chapters of 2 Samuel are unconnected. It is as though the author realized that David's life was virtually over, and all that remained was to pick a significant incident, or a revealing set of circumstances, here or there. In the first book of the Chronicles other such incidents are found.

Why the sudden intrusion of this psalm? It is virtually Psa. **18**, and was probably written some time before this closing period of the psalmist's life. Perhaps it was an old song of praise with which David lived a great deal in these last shadowed days. It certainly contains the deepest and the brightest lessons which life had taught him.

The first was that God could be trusted. He was rock, fortress, deliverer (2), shield, tower, refuge, salvation (3). In the light of this, all the storms of evil which had encompassed David fell into perspective and place (4–7). There follows (8–16) a splendid passage of poetry, which pictures some violent electrical storm in the mountains of the Judean wilderness—

*His chariots of wrath the dark thunder-clouds form,*
*And dark is His path on the wings of the storm . . .*

Such had been life. Like the torrents in the wadis, fed by a wild, mad cloudburst in the hills, violent events had crashed around him, the blows of hostile men and hostile circumstance had been like the stabbing lightning. In the midst of it God had kept His promises (17–22). Only God makes life meaningful and worthwhile. God alone gives it significance (32–49).

So did David survey the past. Life can be best understood in retrospect, and it is good sometimes thus to pause and survey the reality of the plan which has outworked, weaving its perfection out of darkness and light, repaired where wilfulness has tangled the threads, unexpected in its patterns, wondrous in its complexity, and demonstrating a hand that guides and a heart that plans.

Claims to righteousness (23–25) must be seen in the context of the times. There were moral inadequacies, as we have seen, to which David was woefully blind. He was also, however, conscious of the adequacy and finality of the forgiveness which greets true repentance. David's was a character marred by manifold faults, but faults which, until the weakening grip of declining years and wasted mental powers, he was ready to confess—and to one God, the true God, worshipped without taint of heathendom, and understood in clearer perception than many of his contemporaries could show.


## 50 : Araunah

### 2 Samuel 24.16–25; 1 Chronicles 21.18–30; Psalm 68

Araunah and Ornan were the same man. One name was probably Jebusite, the other Hebrew, or a Hebraized form of his name. An ancient gloss suggests that he may have been the last of the royal line of the tribe which had held Jerusalem, until David captured it to be his royal capital.

A threshing floor was always in an exposed and windy place, and that of the Jebusite farmer was on the high ledge of the Jerusalem plateau where the temple was later to stand.

Araunah was no doubt a convert to Yahweh. From the ill-fated Uriah (and earlier) to the honest soldier, centurion Cornelius of Caesarea, the Gentile proselytes of the Bible form a fine company, in a real sense foreshadowing the global Church. Josephus remarks that Araunah was a friend of David, and the fellowship may have dated from the days of David's vigour, when he showed mercy to a defeated opponent.

Look at David's noble word in v. 24. He has met generosity and understanding from an alien, and he responds with like spirit. David is about to pass from the page of history. He has just sinned in pride, for the judgement which fell upon his census-taking activities seems to have been a castigation of pride and arrogance. He has repented of whatever spiritual sin was involved, and now speaks with the authentic utterance of his old devotion. His voice is soon to be charged with words which do not sound like the speech of Psa. **23**. It is good that he put this last abiding word of good into Scripture.

It was curiously fitting that the temple-site should have belonged to an alien. Psa. **68** could possibly have been written at this time, the last poetic utterance of the ageing king. See v. 29 with its suggestion of a wider fellowship than that of Israel. And thus the psalm continues. It is curious how many of the major movements of biblical history find some member of another race associated with the unfolding events. We have met Jethro and Rahab. We shall meet Cornelius and Luke. The message of Col. **3**.11 was apparent for all who could see, from the promise to Abraham on to Isaiah and Jonah. It was difficult to make the Jew see what is meant to be chosen of God. It is difficult to make some people see it today. Araunah was a pioneer. He showed the way.

# 51 : Adonijah

## 1 Kings 1.5–10; 1 Chronicles 3.1–3; 22.17–23.1

Adonijah was David's fourth son (2 Sam. **3**.4; 1 Chron. **3**.1 f.), and, being it seems the eldest living son in the days of David's senility, had some right to expect the succession. Amnon, Absalom, and presumably Chileab, were dead (1 Kings **2**.22). David did not discourage his implied claim to the throne, his assumption of a certain pomp, a bodyguard, and such trappings of royalty. Absalom had indulged in similar self-assertion.

Adonijah must have entertained a certain anxiety over Solomon, because Solomon was the only royal prince not invited to the feast which Adonijah gave presumptuously to his adherents, to whom the nomination of Solomon came as a shock (1 Kings 1.10). According to Adonijah himself all Israel expected him to succeed to the throne.

Two very different men also considered the prince's claims just and lawful. They were Abiathar the high-priest who had followed David faithfully since the days of Saul, when he was the only survivor of Saul's massacre of the priests of Nob (1 Sam. 23.6). He was David's priest in the days of his exile (1 Sam. 23.8–12; 30.7 f.), and a guardian of the ark in the days of Absalom's revolt (2 Sam. 15.24–36). As the last representative of Eli's priestly line, Abiathar may have been an aid to David in reconciling the loosely attached northern tribes to his rule. He may have been the chronicler of the first book of Samuel. That one so experienced supported Adonijah says something for the ability and personality of that prince.

Joab, the army commander, was as experienced a man. His allegiance was deeply significant. Adonijah's failure was due to his haste. David was not dead. He fell a victim to a coup d'etat initiated by the clever Bathsheba and Nathan, whose aid may reflect some religious tension between prophet and priest.

Judged guilty of treason, Adonijah was spared by Solomon, who feared an act of sacrilege (1 Kings 1.51–53), but killed when he asked for the hand of David's nurse, Abishag. Of that more in Study 61. It was a fragile ambition, and the whole sorry scene of grasping haste and unworthy intrigue could have been prevented had David been sufficiently in possession of his wits to organize the succession to the throne on a just and equitable basis.


## 52 : Bathsheba, Nathan and David

### 1 Kings 1.9–53; 2 Timothy 4.1–8

The subtle widow of Uriah, David's old love, has not appeared in the story for a score of years. She is now middle-aged, but is the same clever woman one suspects she must have been when the king was ensnared by her young beauty. She was determined that Solomon should succeed to the throne. It was in tune with David's aged apathy that nothing had been done to secure the succession.

It is possible to sense the hot-house atmosphere of the oriental court into which David's household had degenerated, and thereby to catch some sense of the deterioration the king's own character had suffered. Amid the wreckage of life which surrounded his premature old age, was the ruin of old love. For all the guilt in which that sad liaison began, David had loved Bathsheba, and it is sad to see her enter the royal presence with prostrations (16), like Esther coming before Ahasuerus. She presents her plea with none of the frankness of an honoured wife, but with the subtle and humbly convoluted arguments of the courtier.

An infection surrounded the king. Even Nathan, an old man now, has none of the forthright bravery with which on that earlier occasion he had confronted another David and rebuked his sin. He is part of the palace plot, a figure in Bathsheba's devious intrigue. Nathan, too, found it necessary to use the courtier's arts, and to approach the capricious despot, which David had become, with circumspection. The succession of Solomon was perhaps all along in David's mind. The words of 1 Chron. **22**.17–19 suggest at least that he was commissioned to build the temple, a task surely designed for the royal successor. If so, it was not necessary to come to the king with subtlety and subterfuge. Nor was Abiathar free from reprehensible presumptuousness. A frank report would have been more worthy of Nathan—or perhaps the normal processes of intercourse were no longer possible with the man the moribund David had become.

The scene is a sad one. A man lives too long when he survives his simple manliness, his human dignity, and the sweetness of frank fellowship and unsimulated love. Power had corrupted the shepherd-boy who became Israel's poet king. In mercy, God allowed trouble, and David blossomed briefly afresh. Then the torpidity of the corrupt court wound round him again—and this was the ending. Such an ending it should be our prayer at all costs to be spared. We become that which we entertain at the heart's depths.

Read 2 Tim. **4**.1–8 again and think of another man's ending.

## 53 : David's Death

### 1 Kings 1.1–4; 2.1–10

There was small dignity in David's end. He was about seventy years of age, and might have expected something better than the decrepitude which fell upon him. He had lived a hard life. The years in the wilderness, living in caves and sleeping under the open sky, may have left some physical damage. So too the traumatic experiences of Absalom's revolt, and the arduous struggle to Mahanaim.

He had also known much stress of soul, and suffering had taken its toll of body and of mind. He was a broken man. Winter was on him, chilling his body, in spite of the repulsive measures taken to restore his physical warmth, and chilling his spirit. He was the antithesis of the hale old friend whom O. W. Holmes put into his poem:

*Call him not old, whose visionary brain*
*Holds o'er the past its undivided reign.*
*For him in vain the envious seasons roll,*
*Who bears eternal summer in his soul . . .*

There was no summer in David's soul. He scarcely controlled the present, let alone the past. Out of the past arose ghosts to torment him. He had uttered old words of praise not long before, when Psa. **18**, with its summary of life's experience, had become again his song. But the last slope of life had been a swift descent. In the midst of an exhortation to Solomon to be true, he remembered, to be sure, the beneficence of Barzillai, but he also remembered two rankling hates.

Joab was David's nephew, and had served his uncle well. Unable to deal with a soldier so powerful in his own strength, David leaves Solomon a charge to kill him. Even more base was the sentence on mad, old Shimei, a piece of arrant treachery. 'An old man's past's a strange thing,' wrote John Masefield, 'for it never leaves his mind.' That has elements of truth, but if an old man honours God, he seeks to remember Barzillai and forget Shimei, to keep good alive, and banish evil, lest it be buried with his bones (Job **20**.11). Revenge is a low passion, the pleasure of an abject mind. Curiously enough, as Bacon points out in his essay on revenge, Solomon was to say: 'It is the glory of a man to overlook an offence' (Prov. **19**.11). But here was poor example in Solomon's last memories of his father. To Solomon's credit he tried to spare Shimei, but that is another story.

So the tale ends. We should look to our ending, for in the days when body and brain grow weary, the dark things which, if we allow them, haunt the soul's decaying rooms, creep forth and gain control. To die in honour, love and uprightness, we must allow those things of light and sunshine to flood the soul in the days of our strength.

## Questions and themes for study and discussion on Studies 48–53

1. The Law and human sacrifice.

2. The many-sided trustworthiness of God.

3. Old Testament anticipations of the universality of the Church.

4. The folly of presumption.

5. The corrupting effects of power.

6. What does the Bible say about revenge?

# MAN AND SIN

## A Guilty Rebel: Convicted by the Prophets

### 54 : Sin Exposed

#### Isaiah 1.1–20

In what has been described as a prophetic fly-sheet the nation of Israel is indicted before God because of its apostasy. An appeal is made to witnesses amongst the angelic hosts above and to men on earth (2). Although the references are to the corporate sin of God's people, we cannot fail to be convicted personally by this trenchant denunciation. Sin is subjected to close analysis and is exposed in many aspects.

It is a revolt (2, 5, 20). This was the primal sin of man and rebellion is still of its essence. The word used here stands for the repudiation of authority. It can refer to rebellion against a ruler (1 Kings **12**.19; 2 Kings **1**.1), but in this case it has to do with a child's resistance to parental control. Sin is seen as stupidity (3). Even the less intelligent animals have the sense to know to whom they belong and where their welfare lies, but man is so foolish and ignorant that he refuses to recognize the only One who can help him.

Sin is a burden (4). The nation is loaded with guilt. Its back is broken and it is incapacitated. Sin is evildoing (4). It not only affects the sinner; it injures others. Sin is perversion (4). It involves a departure from God's way and leads to corruption and destructiveness (NEB, cf. Gen. **6**.12). Sin is hereditary, for Israel is addressed as the offspring of evildoers (4, cf. Matt. **3**.7). It is not enough to interpret this as meaning merely that the nation consists of evildoers. It does so by reason of descent.

Sin is desertion (4). The word translated forsaken means abandoned for another god (Judg. **2**.11 ff.; **10**.6, 10; Deut. **31**.16). Sin is contempt (4). God's people have spurned Him. He is the Holy One of Israel but they reckon nothing of that. Sin is alienation (4). The children of God are now cut off from Him because they have turned from Him. Sin is a disease (5 f.). It has infected the body politic from head to foot.

In vs. 10–15 the prophet shows how impossible it is for those who cling to their sin to get right with God through the prescribed ritual. When divorced from righteousness, sacrifice amounts to no more than a bribe. The only hope of sinners lies in the pardoning love of God, if they will but return to Him. For us, too, religious observances and zeal for the church can blind us to our real need.


## 55 : Jerusalem Indicted

### Ezekiel 22

In three successive invectives Jerusalem is condemned for her sins and threatened with judgement. The first of these oracles (1–16) lists the crimes she has committed. The second (17–22) uses the analogy of the smelter's furnace. Israel has become an alloy—no longer pure silver—and the fire of God's anger will melt her people. In vs. 23–31 the fall of the city is fore-shadowed and a roll-call of the guilty is drawn up, including all classes of society.

The sin of Israel reflects the sin of man in every age and place. We will often be reminded of our own fast-deteriorating society as we study this chapter. Sin manifests itself in violence and bloodshed (2 ff., 6, 9, 12 f., 27). Indeed, blood is the keyword of this passage. Jerusalem is a city of blood (3). Its last days before its collapse were marked by murders committed under the pretext of policy as well as the ritual slaughter of children (16.20 f., cf. 7.23; 9.9; 23.37, 39; 24.6, 9; 33.25; 36.18). Disrespect for parents led to a break-up in family life (7). The law required that children should honour both father and mother (Exod. 20.12; Lev. 19.3; Deut. 5.16), and to treat them with contempt was a capital crime (Lev. 20.9; Deut. 27.16).

Injustice was rife. Immigrants were amongst the victims. This is certainly not unknown today. Resident aliens were cheated by extortion (7, 29). Human rights protected by the Jewish law (Exod. 22.21; Lev. 17.8, 10, 13; 20.2) were callously ignored. Orphans and widows—the stock representatives of the deprived and underprivileged—were shamefully treated, again in contravention of the law (Exod. 22.22 ff.).

Informers procured bloodshed by slander (9), despite the prohibition of Lev. **19**.16, and received bribes (12), though this was denounced in Exod. **23**.8.

A sexually permissive society is berated in this comprehensive indictment and our own badly needs to hear these words. To 'commit lewdness' (9) is sometimes a figure for false worship, but in this context is to be taken literally. The expression occurs more often in Ezekiel's prophecy than anywhere else in the Old Testament. The law was explicit in its prohibition of adultery and incest (10 f., cf. Exod. **20**.14; Lev. **18**.7 ff., 15).

At the root of this galloping consumption of sin lay a forsaking of God for idols (3 f.). Here is the source of Jerusalem's defilement. Her people have despised the holy place (Jerusalem Bible) and profaned the holy day (8, 16, 26). They have even consumed idolatrous sacrifices at the mountain shrines declared illegal in the Deuteronomic reform (**6**.3; **16**.16; cf. Hos. **4**.13; Jer. **2**.20). Yet again Scripture insists that man without God is liable to be man without morals.

## 56 : National Sins

### Daniel 9.3–19

Daniel's prayer of confession is one of the most searching to be recorded anywhere in Scripture. It is reminiscent of other passages in its phraseology, although more than simply a mosaic of biblical quotations. It is addressed to God in His might and fearfulness (4a, cf. Deut. **7**.21). The sins of the nation are all the more heinous because they have been committed against One who keeps His covenant (4b).

A series of synonymous verbs in v. 5 indicates the multiplicity and variety of the people's sins. This is not empty repetition. These accumulated expressions suggest that sin is like the fabled hydra with many heads. Daniel acknowledges that 'all Israel' (7, 11) has been involved. God's children have failed to reach His standard, dealt perversely in wilful disobedience, done what is wicked out of inexcusable ingratitude, revolted from Him in irresponsible anarchy (9), and totally ignored His wise decrees. 'Commandments' are the contents of legislation, and 'ordinances' (lit. 'judge-ments') the legal decisions in particular cases which then became binding (5). Refusal to pay heed to God's servants the prophets—the spokesmen of His word—completes the cata-logue of defection (6, 10).

The gist of the confession is contained in v. 7. Daniel freely admits that God is altogether in the right and he and his people are altogether in the wrong. There is no hint of self-justification. They have clearly lost face before God because of their treachery (a strong word, cf. Lev. **26**.40; Ezek. **17**.20). Even though they are aware of God's gracious compassion they nevertheless persist in rebellion (9).

By its infidelity Israel has brought down on itself the divine curse threatened long before (cf. Deut. **29**.20; Num. **5**.21). It is recognized that if God failed to reprimand sin He would be guilty of breaking His promises just as much as if He failed to protect the righteous. How often we purr when we receive God's favours but growl when chastised for sin.

Because of God's invariable faithfulness, Daniel dares to plead for restoration (15–19). It is not on the ground of their own righteousness (18), but only for the sake of God's honour (19). He calls on God to act in accordance with His revealed nature.

Along with Israel, 'Christian' nations have had great privi-leges and have abused them. The Christian cannot shut his eyes to the sins of his own nation, but neither can he stand over against it as if he had no part in its sins. Like Daniel, he will pray from within and will confess 'we have sinned, we have done wickedly'.

# 57 : Sin Next Door

## Amos 1

Amos **1**.3–**2**.3 denounces the sins of Israel's neighbours. In **2**.4–16 Judah and then Israel itself are accused. Greater light brings greater responsibility. These eight woes are all intro-duced by the same formula and follow the same overall pattern. 'Transgressions', as Snaith insists, should be trans-lated as 'rebellious acts'. The Hebrew *peša'* indicates revolt against God Himself rather than an offence against an individual. 'It is part of Amos's message that crime against anybody or anything whatsoever is crime against God' (E. A. Edgehill).

Amos makes no allusion here to ritual lapses. He is concerned with social and national righteousness. His prophecy is characterized by a burning ethical zeal. Men have displeased God by their cruelty, barbarism, contentiousness and belligerency. Sin is nothing short of a rebellion and can on no account be tolerated (Isa. 1.28).

The expression 'for three transgressions . . . . . and for four' (3) suggests the indefinite multiplicity of these enormities. The rabbis taught that three transgressions might be forgiven but that four were beyond the limit. God will not now intervene to avert the inevitable retribution. His word of judgement is irrevocable (cf. Isa. 55.11). The repetition of these solemn warnings in each instance conveys an impression of unrelieved menace.

The order in which the nations are paraded before God to receive their sentence of doom is not that of place or time but of relation to Israel. The grim roll-call starts with Syria, the most oppressive of all Israel's enemies (3 ff.). It continues with the oldest—Philistia (6 ff.)—and then moves to Tyre, with whom Israel evidently had some sort of agreement (9 f.). Edom (11 f.) and Ammon (13 ff.) represented blood relations of Israel. Little does the latter realize, however, that the same inexorable judgement which the surrounding nations have incurred is overtaking them.

Modern history, especially that of Europe, furnishes some amazingly close parallels to some of the sins denounced here. It would be worth reviewing the history of the past few decades in search of parallels as a reminder that the Bible is astonishingly up-to-date and that human nature has not changed. Neither should one's own nation be ignored. We are always much more conscious of others' shortcomings than our own. God would bring us to face them, as He compelled Israel to face hers.

## 58 : Sin at Home

### Amos 2

Like the roll of approaching thunder the successive pro-
nouncements of divine doom draw nearer and nearer to
Israel. Moab is castigated for desecrating the body of an
Edomite king (1 ff.)—perhaps a reference to 2 Kings 3.27.
When judgement reaches Judah, Israel can no longer expect
to escape (4 f.). Neglect of the law and idolatry are common
to both. Perhaps we should recall that under the new covenant judgement is said to *begin* at the house of God.

A series of charges is listed in the actual indictment of
Israel (6–16). Inhumanity, extortion and oppression are included, along with unchastity and apostasy. The instances
cited in vs. 6, 7, however, do not involve the actual infringe-
ment of the law. But the money-mad business men of Israel
craftily used it to serve their own acquisitive ends. We may
keep on the right side of the civil code and yet sin against
both God and man. Our attitude to *people* matters a great
deal to God.

These oppressors would foreclose a mortgage so that the
debtor had to be sold into slavery (cf. Lev. 25.29; Deut.
15.2). While for most of us slavery is a thing of the past, this
kind of sin is not. The title-deeds of some poor man's inherit-
ance would be seized and his land appropriated, if indeed
v. 6b refers to the custom of selling land by the transfer of a
shoe (Ruth 4.7; Psa. 60.8). The rich trampled down the very
heads of the poor in the dust and pushed them aside as they
hurried along the street. It is the underprivileged who invariably suffered, for, as E. B. Pusey pointed out, 'wolves destroy,
not wolves, but sheep'.

The reference in v. 7b is not simply to sexual aberration
but also to idolatry. In the debased religion of the period,
sacred prostitution was part of the ritual pattern. It was a
feature of the Canaanite cults as well as of the Babylonian
temples. It could well happen that father and son resorted
to the same girl. In these pagan shrines, pawned clothes
were used to make rugs on which men prostrated themselves before the altar, and the wine they drank had been
bought with money extorted from the poor (8). The Targum
translates the plural *elohîm* here as 'idols', as if Amos were
distinguishing them from the God of Israel. His name has

been deliberately profaned (7b), but His judgement on sin is imminent (9–16). It is never wise to think of it as remote. 'Behold, the Judge is standing at the doors' (Jas. **5**.9).

## 59 : The Unholy City

### Zephaniah 3.1–8

After announcing judgement on the nations in **2**.4–15, Zephaniah returns in ch. **3** to arraign Jerusalem as he had already done in ch. **1** (cf. vs. 4, 10–13). He castigates afresh the sins that are rampant within all sections of the community, and most especially those in positions of responsibility (3 f.). Leaders are responsible not simply to man but to God, the Governor of all.

Rebellion is set at the head of the crime sheet (1). The people of Jerusalem have defied God and His standards. The verb means to resist insolently. There has been an obstinate refusal to pay any attention to the divine admonition and to submit to discipline (2). The city, moreover, is said to be polluted—no doubt by various sources of defilement, but in particular by bloodshed (Lam. **4**.14; Isa. **59**.3). Our own society is increasingly aware of the dangers of material pollution and increasingly careless of its moral counterpart. Jerusalem, reflecting an enduring characteristic of fallen man, is tyrannical in its oppression and exploitation of the underprivileged classes. The magistrates are so rapacious that they are compared with hungry wolves who devour all their prey as soon as it is killed and leave nothing over for the morning (or perhaps who had 'nothing to gnaw that morning' [Jerusalem Bible], and are thus more than ever voracious in the evening).

Even the religious leaders of Israel have fallen away from God. The prophets who ought to have been His spokesmen are unrestrained in their eagerness to gain cheap popularity (4). Beware the snare of preaching 'to the gallery'! As Jerome explained, 'they spoke as if from the mouth of the Lord and uttered everything against the Lord.' The priests profaned the sanctuary by their impiety and empty ritual and violated the law by twisting it to serve unworthy ends.

Even when God's punitive sanctions were applied men still

persisted in sin (4 f.). What had already befallen Jerusalem should have compelled the citizens to take stock of their condition and return to the Lord. Instead, they only grew more refractory, even rising early to go about their wicked ways. It is because of this deliberate and aggravated disobedience that final judgement will fall.

The root of Jerusalem's sin is disclosed in v. 2b. It sprang from a failure in trust. The prophets unanimously insisted on faith as a *sine qua non* (Isa. 7.9; Jer. 17.7). If we trust God we can no longer place our reliance on self or others.

## Questions and themes for study and discussion on Studies 54–59

1. Isa. 1.1–20 exposes sin in a number of aspects. Complete the list from other biblical references.

2. 'When God is not, everything is changed and everything is allowed' (Sartre). Consider this in the light of the biblical revelation.

3. What other great biblical prayers reveal the intercessor's sense of involvement in the sin of those for whom he prays?

4. Social injustice figured prominently in Amos's indictment of Israel's sin. How far do Christians fail to recognize this factor today?

5. What are the abiding sins of city-life?

# CHARACTER STUDIES

## 60 : Solomon the Great

### Matthew 12.41, 42; Luke 12.27–29

Let us pause before turning in greater detail to the life of
Solomon, to look at the story of his person and his reign as
a whole. He is a contrast with his father David. He began
where David ended. He lived a life of security and peace,
not of war and conflict. He had the vast experience of a
royal father to guide him. He never knew persecution, injustice and rejection.

Solomon had vast advantages. He had wisdom and an
intelligence derived perhaps from his mother. He had, at
first, the gift of humility, the fruit perhaps of Nathan's training. He had such wealth that the Queen of Sheba was reduced
to speechless amazement by his glory. As men measure
earthly monarchy, in terms of frontiers, the land's adornment, and imperial pomp, he was Solomon the Great.

What, we must now ask, did Solomon do with all these
immense privileges, privileges each one of which was a
responsibility? First, he lived a life of self-indulgence. His
sin was genteel and respectable, even within the ambit of
law and custom which allowed an eastern monarch lamentable scope. It was sin, none the less, unrecognized and unconfessed. It begat no repentance. It was vain parade and
flaunted sensuality.

Secondly, his wisdom turned sour in disillusionment, if
Ecclesiastes reflects his later attitude to life. And contrast
that cynical and disillusioned piece of worldly pessimism
with the heart-revealing psalms of David, and even with the
plain wisdom of the Proverbs, so many of which came from
his ready mind and pen.

Thirdly, Solomon had no notion of what the New Testament was to call 'separation' (2 Cor. 6.14–18). The Old
Testament had also been clear enough about the entanglements of fellowship with heathendom. His palace was filled

with heathen women, collected in the pursuit both of carnality and dynastic advantage. His trade with Tyre was to open a sequence of events which led straight to Ahab, and disaster to another generation. Solomon's policies, indeed, were a major contribution to the division of the kingdom, and the sufferings of Israel in the captivities.

## *61 : King Solomon

### 1 Kings 2.10–46

How old Solomon was when he came to the throne is not known. Eumolpus, who allowed him only twelve years, is certainly wrong. So is Josephus, who gave him fifteen. He was possibly nearer twenty. David had yearned for peace. He had called one ill-fated son Absalom, which means 'father of peace'. Solomon's name means 'peaceful'. Nathan, who took an interest in Solomon, called him Jedediah ('beloved of God'), a play on David's own name. Perhaps Nathan brought him up, thus accounting for the old prophet's interest in the succession.

It was 'a close-run thing', but with Benaiah, commander of the household troops, standing by, Joab, the only real danger, was neutralized. There is no doubt that Solomon's own personal ability played a part, for the first recorded events of the reign show him in firm control. It must have been a surprise for Bathsheba when Solomon's deference and courtesy vanished in a flame of anger when she approached him with Adonijah's plea.

Solomon had spared Adonijah, and the request for Abishag in marriage seems hardly sufficient reason for such an outburst, and the deed of blood which followed. Perhaps the move was part of a policy on Adonijah's part which does not appear in the story. If so Bathsheba was unusually obtuse and she was not a foolish woman. Or was Abishag the Shulammite of the Song of Solomon, and did the request fire a blaze of jealousy?

It is revolting to see the new reign begin in deeds of blood and harshness. Abiathar had been forty years a priest, and had served the royal house well. He was dishonoured. Shimei

*Read Studies 61 and 62 together, except during Leap Year.

was put under house-arrest, no doubt because he commanded the sympathy of elements hostile to the throne and loyal to the line of Saul. When it was politic to strike him down, Solomon took the chance. Joab had often enough taken the sword. He perished by the sword, and indeed had earned the capital punishment that David felt incompetent to exact. Grim politics, none the less.

So the tale of the kings begins. Samuel long since had predicted as much (1 Sam. **8**). Said Plutarch, eighteen centuries ago: 'There is no stronger test of a man's real character than power and authority, exciting as they do every passion, and discovering every latent vice'. We shall see illustration in plenty, and the thought that presents itself is that it behoves us all to watch with care how we exercise any authority which falls into our fallible hands.

## *62 : Solomon the Wise

### 1 Kings 3; 2 Chronicles 1

Solomon was a curious mixture. His marriage of convenience with the princess of Egypt was no more than a piece of worldly wisdom designed to bolster his southern frontier while he turned his attention more closely to the more exposed and vulnerable borderlands of his east and north. It grates a little, none the less, to observe the obvious mistakes with which the most materially prosperous age of Israel's monarchy opened.

The worship 'in high places', mentioned by the chronicler with a touch of disapproval, was a feature of the days before the building of the temple, and the Hebrew historian is clearly preoccupied with setting the stage for the great religious project of the reign. The 'high place' was not in itself wrong, but it was a practice of surrounding heathendom, and therefore perilous to religious purity.

Two hereditary forces strove for mastery in Solomon. The dynastic alliance, with the power all the prophets were to preach against, was a piece of carnal shrewdness which one might imagine was a heritage of the cool and calculating Bathsheba. It was not the statecraft of a man of God. The prayer for wisdom, on the other hand, looks more like

David seeking a plan from God in his life. With all his gross faults David desired God's will.

The prayer of Solomon is worth careful reading. There is, to be sure, a due measure of humility and desire for right. Something, nevertheless, is lacking, and perhaps it is a longing for purity and godliness. Solomon looks uncommonly like the rich young ruler who came to Christ. The treasures of heaven lie ready to our hand. Any one of us can take of them according to our choice. We get what we desire. Solomon could have had more than wisdom, good though that desire was, for as Phillips Brooks once said, it is difficult to think of any prayer which God, in giving the answer, might not have wished that we had made larger.

The story which closes 1 Kings 3 shows Solomon at his best. He is wise, indeed, full of human insight, and altogether lovable (27). Here was a man who, had he kept this human touch, might have been one of the great monarchs of all time.


## 63 : Solomon the Wealthy

### 1 Kings 4

Here, indeed, is a spectacle of affluence. Solomon's kingdom was rich and secure. Israel basked in her golden age. The royal figure who presided gloriously over the wealthy nation had nothing to fear from arms upon his settled borderlands. The world respected him, and men came from afar to tap the deep springs of his wisdom. Here was 'Solomon in all his glory'.

But perhaps in his very situation are seen the seeds of decay. A certain temptation lies in ease and in prosperity. Adversity hardens men and nations, purges their minds of many small, mean things. But, as the parable in Deuteronomy had it long since, 'Jeshurun waxes fat and kicks', forgetting the pit from which he was lifted, growing proud and hard.

Thankfulness for the toil of men and the blessing of God, which made the wealth and greatness lying too easily in the hands of men, grows faint. Pride and arrogance take its place. The Greeks used to link three words, which, with some loss of content, may be translated: 'surfeit', 'arrogant behaviour', 'disaster'. The first suggests that demoralization which comes with ease and prosperity and too great success, and the relaxing of the moral fibre which comes to the favoured of fortune. The second word speaks of a loss of moral balance resulting in outrageous confidence, and the conduct which reflects it. The third speaks of the catastrophic result which history shows to be inevitable.

The sequence is too obvious in the history of many lands to be much for our comfort today. We can see its predestined outworking. The moral law, which is interwoven with history, is inevitable in its retributions. This chapter contains no account of sin or calculated wrongdoing. Indeed the king is at the moment contemplating a great building for his God. Nevertheless here is the stage. Here is the framework of ease and security in which Solomon is to feel himself slipping, perhaps slipping without consciousness of what is growing faint in his life. He was a busy man, devoted to the administration of justice, and turning to the pursuits of botany and biology (33) and writing of many things.

## Questions and themes for study and discussion on Studies 60–63

1. A select number of monarchs have become known to posterity by the description 'the Great'. Should we in-include Solomon? What is greatness?

2. The need to keep close to God when we have authority.

3. Wisdom is greater than knowledge, and holiness than both. Can we be *really* wise without being holy?

4. How substantial was the glory of Solomon?

# MAN AND SIN

## A Guilty Rebel: Recognised and Rebuked in the New Testament

### 64 : The Need to Repent

#### Luke 13.1–9

It has to be recognized that, as Earle Ellis points out, 'in the Gospels Jesus does not speak to the question of original sin'. He never discusses it. He simply assumes the universality of sin and regards death as its consequence.

In Luke 13.1–9 an appeal for repentance continues the trend of the previous chapter with its warnings against hypocrisy and contention. Two instances are cited where fatalities had occurred. Although the connection between sin and death is maintained, it is not presumed that the victims were necessarily being punished for any particular offence or that their sin was more heinous than that of others. Indeed, the thrust of our Lord's comment is just the reverse. Unless all repent they too will 'come to the same end' (vs. 3, 5 NEB). If we are spiritually sensitive we should learn lessons likewise from the news items of our day.

Jesus repudiated any doctrinaire theory of retribution. The emphatic negative (3, 5) dismisses Jewish assumptions of this sort. Those who lost their lives in Pilate's massacre (1ff.) or in the accident at the tower of Siloam (4 f.) were not exceptionally wicked. They were ordinary men. Our Lord's purpose is to call His hearers to repentance. He invites them to consider their own sins and their own destiny, rather than to speculate about original sin. Understanding may sometimes need to wait but repentance should never be left until later.

The story of the fig tree in vs. 6–9 urges the need for a speedy response to the grace of God since the time is short. The fact that God is merciful with the sinner must not lead him to take advantage of the divine goodness. God will not wait for ever. The age of grace will eventually close. The expressions 'three years' and 'next year' should not be pressed literally in an application to our Lord's ministry. They simply denote the extension of God's grace (2 Pet. 3.15a). But there is an 'if not' (9). Unless the interval is used for repentance judgement must fall. 'Therefore never send to know for whom the bell tolls: it tolls for thee' (John Donne).

## 65 : The Tyranny of Sin

### Romans 1.18–32

Paul's exposé of human sin and depravity finds its echo today in almost every news bulletin. He begins by describing the original status of man as a being to whom the knowledge of God was revealed. Since then, despite the fall, man has been unable to plead ignorance as an excuse (20, 32). The apostle is not subscribing to some deistic natural theology but recognizing the extent of general revelation.

Sin is here seen as self-determination. It is the promotion of one's own opinions and desires to constitute the norm of conduct instead of seeking the divine will (21). So far from acquiring wisdom by these self-centred speculations, man shows himself to be basically stupid (22). He tends to look down on Christians as naïve and foolish in their belief, but in fact it is he who is so in his unbelief.

Sin is seen as idolatry. Whatever a man cannot live without is his god. The keyword is 'exchange' (23, 25). Something else has been put in the place of God. As a result, man prefers shame to His glory and a lie to His truth. The seat of sin is not to be located in the body but in the self. In the devastating catalogue of enormities from v. 26 onwards the sins of the mind and the soul are included as well as those of the body, as in Gal. 5.19 ff. Verses 24–27 list sins against nature and vs. 28–32 sins against society. It is an oversimplification to equate sin solely with the animal appetites. It may even be a device for evading the Divine condemnation on the sins He hates most—such as spiritual pride.

The result of sin is more sin. That is its immediate penalty. Man becomes an addict. Sin is against God, so God is against sin (18). He abandons man to its effects. Three times over we are told that 'God gave them up' (24, 26, 28). He removes His restraining hand from man and lets licence lead to its own drastic consequences. 'When man does not turn to God, God punishes him by giving him up to sin' (A. Nygren).

## 66 : Secular Morality

### Romans 2.1–16

So far in his indictment of the moral collapse in the Roman Empire Paul would have carried many of his readers with him. As the apostle implies in Phil. **4**.8 f., there were pagans who practised virtues which a Christian must emulate and indeed surpass. They would be as disgusted as we are at the grosser sins of society, but they would claim that they themselves were not implicated. This is the attitude the Jews would take too. Paul deals with them in **2**.17–**3**.20, but in **2**.1–16 he is probably tackling the secular moralists who have their counterparts today.

As K. J. Foreman points out, Paul does not explain his argument nor indeed substantiate it up to the hilt. 'He just tosses out the hand grenade and lets the splinters hit where they will.' Those who regard themselves as ethically superior and who would quickly condemn the moral landslide of the times are in fact guilty of sin themselves (1). Their vulnerability is exposed in a series of questions in vs. 3, 4. Despite their lofty ideals, they are still liable to lapse. They are only storing up the worst sort of trouble for themselves at the end of the age—the wrath of God which cannot condone sin. If God is at present gracious towards them, it is that they may be led to repent. That is the absolute condition of man's reconciliation with his Maker.

Verses 6–11 lay stress on the certainty of final retribution. It is performance that will count at the day of judgement (Psa. **62**.12b). This is not a retrogression to salvation by works. Paul is simply demonstrating the inability of the moralist as such to achieve the righteousness God requires. Apart from the reception of grace in Christ, man is inherently incapable of satisfying God's moral demands, no matter how noble his aspirations may be. Those who choose to be assessed solely on deeds will be condemned by that criterion, for God has no favourites (11).

It is made plain in vs. 12–16 that Gentiles will not be penalized for their failure to observe a code inaccessible to them, but will be judged according to the light they have. Paul does not say that they possess the law, but that its demands are inscribed on their hearts, and their consciences tell them whether they have met its requirements or not.

*A question : Even if I feel relatively secure in reading ch. 1, what is my reaction to ch. 2?*


## 67 : The Depth of Inbred Sin

### Romans 3.1–20

After dealing with a series of casuistical objections raised by Jews in vs. 1–8, Paul proceeds to show that all men without exception are not only subject to the dominance of sin (9) but in fact have actually committed sin (10–18). 'Psycho-analysis confirms what the pious were wont to say', wrote Sigmund Freud, 'that we are all miserable sinners'. In this respect Jews are in no better case than Gentiles, Paul argues.

On scanning the catena of Old Testament passages strung together after a familiar rabbinical fashion, the reader might be tempted to conclude that the verdict is too severe. Not everyone is like that. Paul is not suggesting that they are. 'Total depravity' does not demand that every possible kind of sin should necessarily assemble in each personality. It does imply, however, that all these symptoms of corruption are found in humanity as a whole. In a fallen temple not every block of stone may be broken or defaced in the same way, but each is nevertheless part of the ruin.

As Karl Barth insisted, the doctrine of original sin is not merely one amongst many, but, according to its fundamental meaning, the doctrine which emerges from an honest consideration of history. Men are unaware of what alone can redeem life from its inherent tragedy and bring them true integration and fulfilment. They are blind to the only way that will lead them to peace because they lack any reverence for God (17 f.).

The moral law is universal. It includes all in its condemnation. Every excuse is silenced and mankind is held answerable to God (19). The effect of law is to awaken a realization of sin. But it is incapable of removing it. Hence no man can get right with God along that line. A new method must be found. What it is Paul discloses in the next section (21–26).

## 68 : Disobedience and Disloyalty

### Hebrews 3

Heb. 3.1–4.13 is occupied with God's call to man to enter into His rest. After a reminder in vs. 1–6a that Christ was faithful as a son like Moses as a servant (5), the author stresses the urgency of the call and the response it requires (6b–15). Verses 7–11 contain a quotation from Psa. 95.7–11.

A warning is issued against spiritual obduracy (8). Scripture elsewhere teaches that it is God who hardens men's hearts (Exod. 7.3; Isa. 63.17; Rom. 9.18), and in v. 13 the verb is passive. But it is what Calvin described as 'spontaneous obstinacy', since man contributes to it by assuming that he can trifle with grace. He puts God to the test by venturing as far as he dares into sin without apparent danger. As a result, he becomes like a planet that has wandered from its orbit (10).

The source of such persistent disobedience lies in 'that wickedness of heart which refuses to trust' (Phillips). Disloyalty is implied as well as unwillingness to believe. Some commentators see here at least a verbal resemblance to the evil inclination (*yeser hara'*) of rabbinical literature. The result of such inner distrust is apostasy. Grotius distinguished between two kinds of unbelief: rejection of the truth when it is first presented and, more seriously, after it has been professed. It is this latter which the writer of Hebrews has in mind (cf. 6.1–8). Hence the 'if' in vs. 6 and 14.

The failure of Israel to respond to the divine call is unambiguously attributed to the sin of unbelief (19). *Apistia* (unbelief, 12, 19) is contrasted with *pistos* (faithful, 2, 5). The lesson would not be lost on the readers of Hebrews. They too had experienced God's grace: they too might fail to enter into the promised rest through disobedience (18) and infidelity (19).

The regular use of Psa. **95** in worship in the Anglican communion is salutary. It is good for the Christian to be reminded that the blessings of the New Covenant, like those of the Old, are accessible only to faith, and that he should never become complacent about sin.


## 69 : Sin as Lawlessness

### 1 John 3.4–18

The definition of sin in v. 4 is reversible. Lawlessness is sin and sin is lawlessness. *Anomia* (lawlessness) is in itself a negative concept which indicates a lack of conformity to the revealed will of God. But in Scripture it acquires a positive flavour and denotes active opposition to the law. 'To commit sin is to break the law' (NEB). See Matt. **7**.23; literally 'you who do lawlessness'.

Lawlessness is not, of course, an all-inclusive description of sin. But it serves to reduce it to its basic element. Sin is doing wrong. That stark fact needs to be spelled out unambiguously. This is what makes sin the precise opposite of righteousness. 'The one doing the lawlessness' (4) is contrasted with 'the one doing the righteousness' (7). See v. 10 and **2**.29.

John's readers are fully aware that Christ came into the world in order to remove sins—not merely to bear them but to bear them away. The effect of His atoning death is nullified if we persist in sin (cf. Rom. **6**.1 f.). He is the sinless One who was sent to undo the devil's work (8). Hence the Christian does not make a habit of sin (note the present tense in vs. 6, 9). He may on occasion fall into a single act of sin (**2**.1 aorist), but he never makes a practice of it.

The 'seed' (AV) in v. 9 has been variously interpreted. Moffatt took it to mean children and translated 'the offspring of God remain in him' (i.e. in God). C. H. Dodd and others prefer to see in it the principle of divine life which resides in the regenerate—hence 'God's nature' (RSV). By reference to 1 Pet. **1**.23–25 the seed is linked with the Word of God. But elsewhere in Scripture we find that it is the Holy Spirit who imparts and maintains new life. John confirms this in

v. 24 (cf. **2**.20, 27). We may perhaps adopt Greville Lewis's paraphrase, 'a principle of new life, imparted by God through the Holy Spirit, abides in the man who is born of God.' Hence sin is dealt with not by repression but by displacement.

Sin which is natural in the unbeliever is unnatural in the child of God. To transgress is to go against his renewed nature: 'he cannot sin' whilst he is true to what God has now made him. Sin is a contradiction of sonship (10).

## Questions and themes for study and discussion on Studies 64–69

1. Compile a series of passages from the Gospels illustrating our Lord's call to men to repent.

2. 'The sin of man'; 'the wrath of God against the sin of man'—which is the more appropriate summary of the teaching of Rom. **1**.18–**3**.20?

3. Why should Paul begin the main theological part of 'Romans' in the way he does? What would have been lacking if he had proceeded straight from **1**.17 to **3**.21?

4. Might Heb. **3** and **4** suggest to our minds that restlessness is an element in, or a result of, sin? If so, which?

5. 'Self-coronation, including subtle, unconscious self-coronation—that is the essence of sin' (Vincent Taylor). What passages of Scripture bear out this statement?

6. Consider the relevance of Phil. **4**.8 f. to the question of secular morality. The verb translated 'think about' can also mean 'take into account'.

# CHARACTER STUDIES

## 70 : Solomon the Temple Builder

### 1 Kings 5; Acts 7.47–53

Men's hearts in the quiet cities of Israel were at ease. The land lived in comfort. As yet there was no wide threat of pagan cultic infiltration. The monarch himself was too intellectual a man to be tempted to base and degrading superstitions. Any incursions into idolatry which were to deface his conduct and his reign were indulgences to his wives, the strongest mainspring of his spiritual decay (11.1).

Yahweh, indeed, was honoured with pomp and ceremony, but such obeisance is by no means a guarantee of spiritual commitment or deep truth of worship. The temple was projected in this spirit. Yahweh was an honoured guest, the giver of good things, the architect of all material prosperity. So it seems, if we follow aright in the record the movements of Solomon's mind, that concept of a shrine of beauty took shape. Great building programmes have, through all history, been a feature of 'golden ages', when peace and affluence make available both a work-force and finance. Finance was a matter which fell within Solomon's natural ability. We shall look later at his great trading partnership with the Phoenicians. As expenses mounted, Solomon was not above bartering Israelite territory for northern aid. And the provision of labour led Solomon into tyrannical organization of the working-class of the land. Solomon's weaknesses show here.

The temple itself was Solomon's work, although it found place first in David's mind. It was not specifically ordered of God. It was a laudable project, like the cathedral building of the Middle Ages, and was permitted by God rather than ordained. The tabernacle of Moses' day was in quite another category, and it was full of symbolic instruction. The temple sought to honour God, and that is a worthy desire. The testimony of the Church is not aided by the mean and shabby places of worship tolerated too often by Christian congregations. On the other hand, lavish building can become a hollow symbol. It is what is within the shrine that matters, and gorgeous cathedrals, from Saint Sophia until today, have arisen in ages and in places where evangelism, the prime and indispensable task, have not weighed heavily on the conscience of men. Solomon, in pursuing his dream, neglected much which lay nearer home, as the next generation was to find. Consider, in closing, that other temple, its outward form, and what is within (2 Cor. 6.16).

## 71 : Solomon and Hiram

### 1 Kings 5 and 7

Solomon inherited his father's friendship with Hiram, the Phoenician king of Tyre. The partnership which evolved between them suited both parties admirably, but, although Solomon secured the expensive materials and the equally expensive expertise which his building projects demanded, the Phoenician ruler secured economic advantages of the first order, and it is perhaps no tribute to Solomon's patriotism that he impoverished and denuded his land in the contract.

The Phoenicians, most able of all the Canaanitish tribes, were caught between the Lebanon Ranges and the sea, blocked, in early years, by both Philistine and Egyptian from further penetration south, and unable even to overflow into Galilee and the fertile Esdraelon plain. It was the sea in front, and the magnificent cedar forests behind, which led the Phoenicians to their eminence as ship-builders and traders. What they lacked in their narrow coastal plain was primary produce. They needed the produce of the fertile hinterlands.

Hence the bartering of their timber and craftmanship for wine and oil (5.11). Ezek. 27 gives some idea, from four centuries later, of the diversity and magnitude of the Tyrian and Sidonian trade. In the days of Ahab it was a valuable process of exchange sealed by the dynastic marriage of the young king and Jezebel, to Israel's ruin.

Solomon was the one who initiated this unequal partnership, probably sealing it in similar fashion by a marriage connection. Solomon seems to have patronized deities of Sidon, for his wives' sake (**11**.4), and women of Sidon were among his wives (**11**.5). This gives some substance to Josephus' statement that a daughter of Hiram was in the king's harem. If so it set a sinister example.

Apart from what must have been a valuable payment in primary produce, Solomon also bartered frontier areas of his northern province, twenty Galilean villages (**9**.11–13). There is little doubt that Hiram, genial, diplomatic, brotherly, in fact, got the best of the bargain. His frontier in the south, as Lebanon could wish today, benefited greatly by a buffer zone in Galilee. But Solomon was less than wise to give it.

## 72 : Solomon the Trader

### 1 Kings 9.10–28; 2 Chronicles 8.1–18

We have suggested that in terms of barter and frontier adjustment Hiram had the best of the bargain in the deal with Solomon. But the Hebrews had other wares to offer their northern partner besides farm produce and ceded territory. Solomon commanded access to the Gulf of Aqaba, and the Phoenicians were eager for a sea-route to the rich commerce of the East. It had long been a hemisphere of sea-borne commerce. In the Mohenjo-Daro ruins of the Indus Valley, pottery as old as Sumerian is found. And China traded as far as the African coast. The sea-lanes converged at Taprobane or Ceylon.

It is significant that Solomon must have been aware of this activity and saw the commercial importance of the Gulf of Aqaba. Here he had the better of Hiram. The ships that traded to Ophir, which was Southern Arabia (**9**.28), and which rode the monsoons to India (**10**.22)—if we may guess their destination from the cargoes—were big seagoing traders called 'ships of Tarshish', from Tartessos in Spain, whither the Phoenicians sent for tin. 'China clippers' of the last century, and 'East Indiamen', of the century before, did not necessarily trade to China or India.

Solomon controlled the ships and paid the Tyrian skippers,

Hence the apparent discrepancy between 1 Kings 9.28 and 2 Chron. 8.18. Solomon hired expert shipmen from the north. Doubtless he paid them liberally. (See again 1 Kings 5 for the careful arrangements he is likely to have made in his maritime venture also.) The difference between 420 and 450 is $6\frac{2}{3}\%$. It seems likely, then, that the discrepancy between the two accounts gives us the amount of the total salary bill of Solomon's Tyrian officers. One writer apparently records the value of the specie shipped at Ophir. The other gives the figure for the net amount paid into the Jerusalem treasury.

As we probe the accounts for Solomon's character, we encounter an able intellectual. His roving mind had a grip on foreign policy, and the international scene. He saw Israel as one of a company of nations, with a part to play, with peace to keep, with wealth to garner. Perhaps his concept of the nation was not unlike that of modern Israel. The mystic vision has faded. It was to be born again, not in affluence but in adversity. And the seeds of that adversity were sown by the clever, worldly-wise man who was born of Bathsheba.

## 73 : Solomon's Temple

### 1 Kings 6; Jeremiah 7.1–11

Solomon's temple revealed something of the man. What a man builds often shows the nature of the builder, and the temple was a notable expression of a tremendous and consuming personal ambition. It was not a large building by some standards, but it was mightily founded, and rich beyond any other building in the world at that time.

The tabernacle of Moses' day was a light impermanent structure of exquisite craftsmanship. God asked for beauty and wealth to adorn His desert shrine. The temple of Solomon was a burden to the land. It was perhaps from his Egyptian father-in-law, Dean Farrar suggested, that Solomon learned the employment of forced labour, which the temple demanded. The free people of the land provided a work-force in the forests of the Lebanon to an extent which must have disrupted family-life and distorted the economy. In their Egyptian bondage the people of Israel had known what it was to toil for the taskmaster. Now they learned to endure the burden in their own land (5.13–17). The remnants of Canaan, the 'strangers within the gates', bore an inhuman load (9.20 f.). The smoke stains are visible on the walls and roofs of the quarries whence these serfs hewed the cyclopean stones which the temple demanded—and all the rest of Solomon's building projects. As has been pointed out, for all the elaborate nature of its symbolism, the temple was not a sumptuous building. Solomon had much on his programme besides, and the labour and wealth of Israel were turned to this end. Like Pericles, like Augustus, he immortalized himself in stone. And the land must have groaned under the burden.

Three times a year, we are told (9.25), Solomon officiated at sacrifice, apparently in person, the breach of ritual which was accounted sin in the case of Uzziah (2 Chron. 26). This act was in itself an indication of what the shrine meant to Solomon, a framework within which his very formalities of worship were accounted an exhibition of his royal pomp and estate.

Solomon was permitted to build his temple. Like any act of man it could have been a sign of devotion and true worship. God owned it to that extent, and Solomon was given every encouragement to make his temple a symbol of his allegiance to his God. But the temple, apart from what it stood for, counted for nothing. The display of human wealth means nought to God. Neither Solomon's shrine, nor the two which followed it on the same site, were ever more than material symbols, of value and meaning only in so far as they measured a spiritual reality. From Jeremiah to Stephen this truth is made clear.

## 74 : Solomon's Prayer

### 1 Kings 8 and 9

It has been said that two natures seem to strive in Solomon. In his prayer and sermon at the dedication of the temple, he echoes his psalmist father, and in the closing movement of his prayer joins the prophets. He gives voice to the ancient vision of Abraham, of a world brought to worship the One true God because of His doings in the national life of one people.

A wondrous ideal possessed Solomon's brilliant mind that day (8.54–61), a land blessed and tranquil in the lap of God's peace. There are few scenes of such rest and quietness in the Old Testament. War and rumour of war, menace, bitter strife and harsh captivity, fill its pages. The message of the book was often wrought out behind frontiers of fear. The quiet and happy land of Solomon's blessed vision depended upon faithfulness, gratitude and pure devotion. But Jeshurun, as we quoted before, 'waxed fat, and kicked . . . forsook God who made him and scoffed at the Rock of his salvation' (Deut. 32.15)—and there came to pass the fears of Solomon's prayer, and redemptive disaster.

Here was the acme of Solomon's glory. The dedication of the shrine he had built, for all the toil and sweat and blood and tears which went into its building, seems to have been a time of deep spiritual experience for him. He spoke words of resounding truth, and touched the edge of prophecy. God took his words (9.1–9) and pressed them home upon his spirit. The great king, at this moment, could have been the great priest and prophet of his people.

It is clear that Solomon fell short of this ideal, and lost this appealing opportunity. What went awry? He ended in philosophic pessimism and under the chronicler's rebuke. The latter half of ch. 9 perhaps provides the key. Others had laboured, and Solomon entered into their labours. He lived in affluence. There was little soldiering for him to undertake (2 Chron. 8.3), for the frontiers were secure. The good things of life began to hold and to preoccupy a man of taste, culture, education and strong carnality.

Solomon became an eastern monarch. The people accepted him in such a role, for he had, after all, brought them peace. They lay in willing servitude, like the people of Rome when Augustus gave them ease. This is not health. It is an Indian Summer of a nation's life and the winter is soon to follow. As Milton says in *Samson Agonistes*:

> *But what more oft in nations grown corrupt*
> *And by their vices brought to servitude,*
> *Than to love bondage more than liberty,*
> *Bondage with ease than strenuous liberty.*

## 75 : Solomon's Guest

### 1 Kings 10; Revelation 3.14–19

Solomon's fragile glory meant nothing to Christ. He set it lower than the adornment of the flowers of the field. It meant much to the nations which the king sought to influence. His reputation travelled with his trade, and that seems to have reached the Malabar coast. Sanskrit roots lie behind the words for 'ivory and apes and peacocks', which came back with his cargoes, and they seem to be Tamil words which speak of South India.

Both by sea and along the desert camel-ways, his fame also went down to Shabwa in the Yemen, where the extensive remains of an ancient culture await the caprice of a government which forbids exploration. The Queen of Sheba, Balkis by name, according to tradition, heard of the glory of Solomon and travelled up the caravan-routes to Jerusalem to visit him, and set a hundred stories of wonder and romance circulating in the legends of Arabia, Ethiopia and Israel.

She saw the material prosperity of the Hebrew court, the wealth of its services and adornments, the pomp and circumstance of the king, and she was overwhelmed by it. She blessed God (9) for the beneficence which had heaped such wealth at the feet of one astute young man, and if Sheba's queen gained anything of worth from her visit, it was not the loads on her returning camels of Solomon's rich gifts, but this faint insight into the Hebrew faith. It might have been a deeper and more salutary conception had Solomon rather impressed her with his worth and righteousness and the depth of his devotion to God. The irony was that all the wealth which the queen admired was to feed the spoiler. Israel had really more to offer.

Did some conception of the land's destiny travel back down the desert roads in the minds and hearts of more sensitive members of the royal train? Did it find root there, and, over nine centuries later, send some watchers of the skies up the same long highways, following a star to Bethlehem?

Solomon is a pathetic figure in this chapter, robed in his glory and posing before the Sabaean queen. He looks like Haroun al Raschid of the *Arabian Nights,* or like some Charlemagne or Montezuma. Dean Stanley put it well: 'That stately and melancholy figure—in some respects the grandest and the saddest in the Sacred Volume—is in detail little more than a mighty shadow. Of all the characters in the Bible he is the most purely secular; and merely secular magnificence was an excrescence, not a native growth of the chosen people.'


## 76 : Solomon the Philosopher

### Ecclesiastes 1, 2, 11 and 12

The writer of Ecclesiastes calls himself 'the Preacher'. He remarks that he was a king of Jerusalem, but nowhere actually says that he was Solomon. Old tradition, however, maintains that Ecclesiastes was Solomon, and if, indeed, the language is such that it precludes so early a date, the fact may be that the book was modernized, as we today modernize its translation, without losing its significance or context. If another was 'the Preacher', the book could be built round remarks of Solomon such as 'vanity, all is vanity' and many others which could not now be disentangled from the text.

Solomon fits the context. He was a prolific writer, on botany and biology, as well as on ethics. Two hundred of his three thousand proverbs survive, even if the whole collection of the Proverbs of the Old Testament is not his. The ancient world spoke of psalms attributed to him, but none survives.

But turn to Ecclesiastes as a possible final distillation of what Solomon drew from life. What is its possible significance for us? It is manifestly not a text book of biblical ethics or philosophy. 'Be not righteous overmuch' (Eccl. 7.16) is in tune neither with the Old Testament nor the New. Gloom and pessimism, mixed with a fatalistic theism, reign in the Preacher's pages. He writes like Euripides and Lucretius rather than like Isaiah. Should the book then appear in the Scripture canon? By all means. It is a record of man's mind. It is the famous wisdom of Solomon the Wise in its utmost human reach, and full of its own inadequacy. It shows us what the brilliant king was in the days of the disillusionment which followed his overdrinking of the cup of his rich life.

Faith and holiness are not ingredients in his sad philosophy. Set his book over against his father's psalms. Solomon's page is bitter with much thought. In David's verse there are heart-beats and the spirit's striving. In the completeness of the Old Testament both records are relevant. 'Fear God,' concludes the Preacher. David feared, but loved as well. The sum of things is vanity indeed, but faith can find another world.

## 77 : Solomon the Moralist

### Proverbs 1 and 8

It is impossible to say how many of the proverbs in the book that goes by that name were products of Solomon's own wisdom, for 1.1 does not provide a heading for the entire book. The author in each case does not matter. Bearing in mind that it is the men and women of the Bible, their character and personality, which we are here seeking, let us ask what manner of man it was who gave such stimulus to the collection of wise sayings and crystalized wisdom.

A preoccupation with such literature dates to earliest times. Jotham's fable (Judg. 9.8 ff.), Samson's riddle (Judg. 14.14 and look at Prov. 1.6), Nathan's parable (2 Sam. 12.1 ff.), are examples of this style of speech and this pre-occupation with ethics in a practical form. Such thought, and its associated literature, were an offshoot of religion, a movement of the mind born of Israel's passion for justice.

It was natural that an intellectual like Solomon should find a deep interest in the polished and sharpened conclusions of religious thought. The danger in such personalities is that a concentration on these matters, and the codes of conduct which so readily take shape from them, will form a substitute for that love of God, that committal of heart and mind to His will, and that spiritual devotion, which is true godliness.

Wisdom, as man sees it, can be alien from 'the fear of the Lord' which is the true beginning of wisdom (9.10. See Gen. 3.6). On the other hand, in Deuteronomy we read (4.6) of the Law as being Israel's 'wisdom and understanding in the sight of the nations'. Solomon demonstrates both situations.

Perhaps wisdom turned dry and sour as the years went by, and became the pessimistic philosophy of Ecclesiastes. In earlier years he perhaps saw deeper into spiritual truth, and we catch another glimpse of what the clever monarch might have been. Observe some of his penetrating insights—his understanding of what the Lord was to call the 'unpardonable sin' (**29**.1), his conception of the prophets' office in the same chapter (**29**.18), and his preview of 'the Word' of John's Prologue in the fine chapters on Wisdom (**8** and **9**).

Dr. Billy Graham is said to read a chapter of the Proverbs each day. Whoever does so, whatever the diversity of authorship may be, has notable contact with Solomon's mind. To gain an impression of that mind's worth and power, the exercise might be worth while.

## 78 : Solomon the Poet

### Song of Solomon 1, 2, 7 and 8

The Song of Solomon is probably an utterance of the royal poet's young manhood. It would be difficult to believe that the ardour of love which it expresses could have survived the blighting presence of a harem, and Solomon's band of casual 'wives'.

The song may be fairly and simply regarded as a lyric of love. Sub-Christian asceticism, loath to believe that God's benediction could rest so frankly on physical love, allegorized the poem. One rabbinical school took it to be a representation of God and His loved Israel. Catching up this thread of thought, Christian interpreters have declared the song to be an allegory of Christ and His bride the Church. For most sensitive Christians this creates difficulties. The rich and ardent language, replete with the facts and symbols of physical love, repel when applied to the mystic union of the Lord and His Church.

It is best to look upon this wild poetry as the sanctification of the love of man and woman. It holds that place in the Old Testament which the story of Cana and its wedding holds in the New. The intensity and wealth of the language speak of a Solomon not yet sated with life, but meeting a beloved bride and receiving in return the uninhibited response of a devoted love.

The details of interpretation, the nature of the dialogue, whether some drama is interwoven with the poetry, the identity of the bride, these and other facets of meaning need not here detain us. What we seek is the poet rather than his poetry. We meet a mind rich in its imagination. The imagery, prior to the psychological extravagances of modern poetry, might have seemed remote and alien to Western poetic tradition, formed by the reserve of classicism and lacking the ardour of the East.

Therein lies the interest. Solomon, the cool intellectual, was also a romantic, pouring unrestrained feeling into coloured and exotic speech which reflected the free, unreasoning passion of a youthful love. There was no shame in such encounter, for there was no call for shame. The pity is that it was too probably a fire which died of its own heat, or stifled in the hot-house atmosphere of the Eastern court in which the best of Solomon was lost.

## 79 : Solomon's End

### 1 Kings 11.1–25, 41–43; 1 Samuel 8.10–18; Deuteronomy 17.14–20

Solomon knew what a good king should be, and should do. He had revealed that knowledge in the great Dedication Prayer. It was also set down twice in Scripture what abuses might follow a base interpretation of royalty. And if Deuteronomy had been lost, not to be discovered until Josiah's day, Samuel's warning must have been among the priestly records of the land. Solomon with his pomp and selfish wealth fulfilled all the dire warnings of the last of Israel's judges.

All, indeed, was vanity, as Solomon drew near his end. Polygamy always carries a curse, and despotism has a rotten-ness at its core. Solomon set the example, which Ahab was to follow, of importing paganism along with his pagan women. His wisdom, as well as his carnality, played him false. It was dynastically expedient, he reasoned shrewdly, to link foreign thrones with his by marriage. Spiritually it was disastrous.

The first sign of falling shadows came in the latter years of his reign. Hiram seems to have drawn away from his old friend. He had a goodly bargain in the frontier adjustments in Galilee, but for some unexplained reason was angry about the ceded territory (1 Kings **9**.11–13). Probably Solomon withdrew the Hebrew population, and stripped the surrendered districts of their amenities. Economically Israel was in a bad way. Hence the meaning of the cryptic remark about Hiram's talents of gold (**9**.14). It was probably a well-secured loan. Solomon had offended against the Law by alienating such tracts of land as the abandoned sector of Galilee (Lev. **25**.23 f.).

It had been a time of peace, thanks to David's vigorous ordering of the frontiers. Now came the shadow of war, as the frontier peoples began to realize that the golden age was paling to its end. We catch in the last chapter of Solomon's record the miasma of Ecclesiastes. Life had become a magnificent monotony. 'Solomon in all his glory' was to become a legend. Like Midas, in whose hand all things turned to gold, Solomon had won all that life could give him in pleasure, in material things. He was now in his middle fifties, and life was virtually done. There is a moral law whose sanctions cannot be avoided. Solomon was wise enough to know that fact. His backsliding was no fault of ignorance. But he was a lonely man. No bold Nathan rebuked him. The insincerities and servile flattery of an artificial court ringed him round and walled him from the truth. He moves out of the page of history leaving troubles behind him. He had, like Demas, loved this present world, and loved it too much . . .

> *That luxurious king, whose heart, though large,*
> *Beguiled by fair idolatresses, fell*
> *To idols foul . . .*

(Milton)

Solomon was about fifty-eight when he died.

**Questions and themes for study and discussion on Studies 70–79**

1. Church building—its purpose, its goal, its abuse.

2. The temple in the New Testament.

3. How far can the Church employ the skills of the world?

4. The perils of affluence.

5. Why was Solomon allowed to build the temple when David was not?

6. Why does philosophy so often end in pessimism?

7. Which of Solomon's proverbs seem most relevant today?

8. Religion and the intellectual.

9. Marriage and backsliding.

# MAN AND SIN

## A Helpless Slave

### 80 : Inner Uncleanliness

### Matthew 15.1-20

The rite of purification was regarded by the legalistic Jewish leaders as a test case to distinguish between piety and laxity. They suspected that Jesus was not sound on this matter. A deputation arrives from Jerusalem to question Him about His disciples' behaviour. Our Lord does not give a direct answer. Instead He challenges the whole system of externalism.

He exposes the hypocrisy of His critics by showing that in fact they themselves only pay lip-service to the law when it suits their book (5 f.). They are ready to contravene the fifth commandment for the sake of a rash vow (itself regarded as incurring guilt in Lev. 5.4). This is nothing short of idolatry, for it allows traditional authority to usurp God's rightful place.

Then in vs. 10-20 Jesus deals with the underlying question of defilement. He insists that it is not primarily ceremonial but moral. It is the inward disposition not the external appearance which disqualifies a man from fellowship with God. Uncleanness comes from within and not from contacts without. It is not what goes into the mouth which defiles, but what comes out of it.

Jesus had spoken in a guarded way, although the lesson He intended to convey was plain enough. The disciples, however, demand a fuller explanation and in vs. 17-20 our Lord spells out unambiguously what He meant. Without actually speaking of sin He shows how it finds expression in the offences listed in v. 19 which infringe the commandments from Six to Nine. Evil thoughts lead to murder (6th.), adultery, fornication (7th.), theft (8th.), perjury and slander (9th.). This is the real source of uncleanness. Merely to omit the ablutions prescribed by tradition (not by the law itself) does not necessarily imply a sinful condition (cf. Luke 11.37–41). The most serious defilement is moral rather than ceremonial. Jesus could hardly have more forcibly stressed the inwardness of sin and the need to cleanse the central springs of human personality (Prov. 4.23; Jer. 17.9).

*Questions: What elements of externalism exist in contemporary religious life which tend to hinder the recognition of man's inner uncleanness? How can the situation be remedied?*


## 81 : The Way of Salvation

### 1 Corinthians 1.18–31

Paul is dealing with God's method of salvation. He contrasts the false wisdom with the true. The message of the cross reaches two classes of men: those who are on the way to destruction and those who are on the way to salvation (18). There is a clear-cut distinction here. It is the consistent insistence of Scripture that all of us must be either saved or lost. There is no third category, no half-way house between heaven and hell. As Jesus Himself taught, the broad way leads nowhere but to destruction (Matt. 7.13). To take it is the height of folly.

From v. 20 to v. 25 the apostle shows that even human wisdom (let alone human folly) is incapable in itself of conveying the knowledge of God. Corinth, like all Greek cities, would have its share of philosophers and other intellectuals. Our slavery of sin touches every part of our nature. Our minds are affected by sin, because any thinking which does not begin from God (not simply the general conception of deity, but the recognition of the true and living God) is bound to go astray in some way. 'Earth-bound' thinking is thinking in bondage. Types of thinking may change and the Platonism and Stoicism of the Greeks may be out of fashion today, but modern existentialism with its stress on the individual's quest for self-fulfilment falls just as much under the judgement of the cross.

The truth is that God has designed only one way of salvation, and no other. The cross was not brought in as an afterthought. It was the ordained means of redemption from the beginning. An offence to sign-seeking Jews and nonsense to philosophical Greeks, Christ crucified is in fact both the power and the wisdom of God (22 ff.). God's apparent foolishness and weakness are superior to human wisdom and strength (25).

In the final paragraph Paul provides a window on the church in Corinth. Here is a breakdown of its composition in terms which would nowadays fascinate any sociologist. Not many intellectuals, not many of the influential, not many aristocrats, are to be found in the congregation. According to the world's standards it is an assembly of nonentities. But God can use the lowest of the low, and even 'those who are nothing at all, to show up those who are everything' (Jerusalem Bible).

## 82 : Freedom from Sin

### Romans 6.1–14

The questions in v. 1 were suggested by the closing paragraph of the previous chapter (5.18–21). The one trespass of Adam multiplied into the many trespasses of his descendants. Are we therefore to infer from this that our sins are to be increased in order that we may gain further opportunities for God's superabundant grace to be displayed? Paul's own initial hostility to the gospel had been met with overflowing grace (1 Tim. 1.13). Should we then deliberately plunge into sin in order to achieve a similar result?

Such antinomian policies are altogether inconceivable. We are not to do evil so that good may come (3.8). The Christian no longer lives in sin. He must not take advantage of God's grace. 'God will forgive me. It is His trade,' said Heine on his deathbed. But, as Foreman reminds us, God is not a vast forgiving machine. Justification is not the last word of evangelical doctrine. In its biblical content it is inseparable from sanctification. The Christian's baptism symbolizes his death to sin so that he might be raised to new life in Christ (4).

'With him' is the clue to the section from vs. 5–11. The old self was nailed to the cross with Christ. The body, of which sin had formerly taken possession, is no longer en-slaved by sin. So far as sin's approach is concerned, it has been put out of commission. It is no longer at sin's disposal. This liberation from sin's bondage is achieved by death. When a man dies he is released. But Paul here transcends any courtroom concepts. He has moved to an entirely new dimension. This freedom from sin is made possible by the death of Christ. In Him a victory has been gained 'that needs no second fight and leaves no second foe'.

In 5.17 death reigned because of Adam's transgression. Here Paul pleads that sin may no longer reign, since Christ has died (12–14). It would be futile to urge sinners not to let this tyrant oppress them unless the news could first be con-veyed that he has already been overcome. It is in our mortal bodies that sin still attempts to gain control. This mortality was brought about by original sin and will remain. The possibility of conquest is offered even within the limitations of the flesh. Sin need not lord it over us. In the sphere of grace, it can be subdued.


## 83 : Release from Slavery

### Romans 6.15–23

The question raised in v. 1 is repeated and reconsidered. Paul employs an analogy from slavery in order to illustrate the Christian's release from the domination of sin. If we are to appreciate its force we need to understand something of the place of slavery in the Roman empire. When a master bought a slave, he took him over completely. There was nothing the slave could call his own. He was in complete subjection. Such is the condition of the natural man with respect to sin.

Paul points out that this is how we once were (17, 20). We persistently presented ourselves as the serfs of sin (16, 19). It was a willing obedience. But all we got out of it was spiritual death. 'Fruit' is only used by Paul in a good sense (Gal. 5.22; Eph. 5.9; Phil. 1.11). It is the works of darkness which are unfruitful (Eph. 5.11). No worthwhile harvest can be gathered from the service of sin.

The Christian, on the other hand, is emancipated from this

slavery (18, 22). This is the release from bondage which restores man to the status he lost in the fall. Sin has usurped the authority which really belongs only to God (5.12 f.). We were never meant to be in chains. God created us for freedom in dependence on Himself. We might expect Paul to contrast the bondage of sin with the liberty of the righteous. Instead, paradoxically, he speaks about the new delightful submission involved in being a slave of Christ (18 cf. **1**.1). To regard this simply as an unfortunate paradox is to overlook the biblical insistence that man's truest freedom springs from his obedience to God.

For the Christian there is a genuine harvest. The return he gets is sanctification (22). It leads to life everlasting—the opposite of death in v. 21. Both begin now and determine the future. Verse 23 offers a threefold contrast between wages and gift, death and life, sin and God. Sin is a master who pays his slaves with death. This is the grim recompense incurred by Adam's first disobedience, but not paid out until the end. 'The servant of sin gets the only wages sin can pay' (G. R. Cragg). The free gift of God in pure grace is eternal life. Whereas the result of sin passed automatically to all men, the gift of God procured by the death of Christ becomes ours only through faith.

## 84 : Anatomy of Sin

### Romans 7.7–25

In this piece of autobiography Paul analyses his own experience of sin and his struggle to master it. Some commentators take vs. 7–13 as referring to his condition before conversion, and vs. 14–25 as reflecting his conflict even as a Christian, although perhaps only a carnal one (14). But others contend that there is still much to be said for the interpretation of the early Church which related the whole passage to Paul's pre-conversion reaction to the law. Verses 7–13 then allude to his state before he was confronted by the challenge of God's moral demand, whereas vs. 14–25 describe his tragic dilemma as an earnest Pharisee, knowing full well what he ought to do yet finding himself quite incapable of achieving it.

The first paragraph deals with the dawn of conscience. The link between the law and the origin of sin is recognized as in 1 Cor. **15**.56. It is the law which makes man aware of the distinction between good and evil, and thus sets the stage for the contest which Paul describes (7, cf. **3**.20). It is noticeable that the apostle focuses attention on the tenth commandment with its prohibition of covetousness. This is the one requirement of the Decalogue which penetrates beneath the surface of man's conduct and examines his inner motivation. Jesus was to do the same with respect to other commandments (Matt. **5**.21 f., 27 f.).

Law also stimulates the desire to sin (8 f., 11, 13). It provides sin with a base of operations. So sin springs to life again and resumes its murderous work. The false security of the ignorant sinner is disturbed by the law. He realizes that he is facing a killer (11). Sin is out to slay, and the effect of the law is to make him aware of its lethal intentions. It reveals the deadly nature of sin and the sheer inability of even the most morally determined of men to break loose from its fatal grip. The fault, as Saul the Pharisee had discovered, lay not in the law as such, which was all that it should be in itself (12), but in his own sin-bound nature (14). Hence the frustration expressed so agonizingly in vs. 15–20.

K. E. Kirk described vs. 17–20 as 'a parenthesis on the lower self'. Paul is dealing not only with flesh but actually with sin (17, 20). Verse 24 is a cry from the heart echoed by all who are prepared to face the truth about themselves. The deliverance for which Paul longs is not from his body as such, but from that which subjects his body to death through the power at work in his members, namely, the principle of sin within. A present though not final emancipation is assured in Christ (24 f.) and made possible by the Spirit (**8**.2 ff.). On this interpretation v. 25b simply summarizes the state of things before this intervention.

*A thought : The most noticeable word in this passage is 'I'. What can I learn from that?*

## 85 : Man's Natural Condition

### Ephesians 2.1–10; 4.17–19

In the Greek 2.1–10 forms one long sentence. It deals with the remarkable quickening which takes place in the life of one who is delivered from the slavery of sin and shares the victory of Christ. The opening verses describe the plight of such a man before the work of the Spirit begins. This is how the Ephesians and we ourselves•once were—spiritually dead and alienated from God (1). Our condition was brought about by our rebellious acts and our sins. The two terms ('trespasses and sins') are used in combination to stress the gravity of this cause of our spiritual death, and the plurals indicate the continuity of its effect.

This was the sphere we formerly occupied. We took the way of the world and lived in terms of this present evil age. We were under the control of Satan, who is represented as the unholy spirit (2). As Christians are filled with the Holy Spirit and directed by Him, so those who rebel against God are activated by the evil spirit. Our old life was dominated by the desires arising out of our fallen nature. As Paul declares in Rom. 7.18, nothing good dwells in the flesh. Here then is our natural state—we are subject to God's wrath and fury (Rom. 1.18; 2.5, 8).

Wrath and fury are the unvarying reactions of God's holiness and righteousness against sin. He cannot condone it if He is to be true to Himself. 'By nature' (3) refers to inbred sin. Although the word (*physis*) may sometimes imply that which is habitual (and so 'second nature', as we say), it is regularly used to indicate what is innate. This is human nature at its conception and birth (Psa. 51.5). Paul is alluding to what is commonly known as original sin—man's congenital depravity as taught throughout Scripture. What is born of the flesh is flesh and thus tainted from the start (John 3.6). Verses 4–10 proceed to speak of the quickening the Spirit brings.

In the other passage (4.17–19) we have a further reference to the conduct of unbelievers. The Ephesians are urged to avoid the behaviour of the Gentiles who are cut off from God because of their inability to comprehend spiritual truth (18). This is not the ignorance of those who have failed to accept knowledge: it is an inborn ignorance which results from original sin. Hence their intellect is blinded and the heart grows callous to spiritual influences. This blunting of the moral sense leads to permissive behaviour of every kind. Futility (17) marks all that we did as unregenerate. The word means that which fails to lead to the goal. Unbelievers are off course in life. They will never find happiness and integration. They are engaged in a wild goose chase which gets them nowhere. What a contrast to the fulfilled life of the Christian!

## 86 : Strife Within and Without

### James 4.1–10

There is a startling transition from 'peace' (3.18) to 'wars' (4.1). What follows sounds like an account of our belligerent and acquisitive society today. But man has always been like this. Sin expresses itself in much the same way in every generation.

The reference in v. 1 is to private quarrels rather than to international wars. There is strife between man and man because there is strife within each man. We are ourselves by nature a walking battle-ground, and this inner conflict is perpetuated and indeed aggravated in our social relationships. If we cannot live at peace with ourselves, we are hardly likely to live at peace with others (cf. Rom. 7.23; 1 Pet. 2.11).

Man continuously craves for what he does not possess. There is a persistent voice within him which cries, 'I want.' When life replies, 'You can't,' he stamps his foot and shouts, 'I must, I will.' Here is what underlies our unrest today. The endless procession of desire, frustration and violence within unredeemed human nature has already been mentioned in 1.13–15.

Verses 4 f. constitute a sharp aside. James turns on his readers and accuses them of being as faithless as adulterous wives. Sin is represented in terms of marital infidelity. To make the world our friend is to make God our enemy. It is impossible to serve God and mammon (Matt. 6.24). Love both for the world and God are incompatible with each other (1 John 2.15).

120

Verse 5 is a puzzling one. No actual Scripture says what is recorded here, although several passages are in line with it (Gen. 6.5; 8.21; Prov. 21.10). Calvin bemoaned the fact that the text had worried many interpreters and had been worried by them! Perhaps it is preferable to punctuate the verse somewhat differently and thus obviate the question of direct quotation altogether. 'Do you think the Scripture is meaningless when it speaks on this subject (i.e. worldliness)? No: God yearns jealously over the spirit He has set within us.' If this is indeed the correct interpretation, then we realize how solicitously God watches over every man.

Despite man's rebellion, God continues to pour out the abundance of His grace. It is those who are prepared to give in to God who will be enabled to withstand the evil one (7).

## 87 : Advice for Transgressors

### James 4.11–5.6

The apostle's mood suddenly changes at 4.11 from denunciation of sin to reasoning with the sinner. He pleads with his readers to realize what they are doing when they indulge in malicious criticisms of one another, and his words are applicable to us also. When we do this we are in fact presuming to set ourselves above the law and in so doing we bring it into disrepute.

James probably has in mind the royal law of love (2.8) which, as interpreted by Jesus, goes beyond the bare demands of Mosaic legalism. Any attempt to denigrate a brother in Christ represents an affront to the supreme ideal of love. To judge another is more than merely foolish. It amounts to spiritual arrogance of the worst sort. We usurp the divine prerogative when we pass judgement on others. The stern warning of Matt. 7.1 must have haunted James' memory, for how could he ever forgive himself for the way in which he had judged Jesus (cf. John 7.3 ff.)?

In v. 13 the apostle confronts a different group. He rebukes those who fail to recognize that all life is under the providence of God. He addresses the business men of his time who have succumbed to the canker of materialism. The spiritual dimension has disappeared from their calculations. In their preoccupation with their business activities they proceed to arrange their schedules as if there was no God to reckon with. James might have been writing about today's commercial rat race! 'Great God, whither is man fallen?' wrote Thomas Mann. 'First we practise sin, then defend it, then boast of it. Sin is first our burden, then our custom, then our delight, then our excellency!'

In v. 17 James enunciates a general principle. If I know what is right and yet fail to do it, then for me that omission is sinful. No amount of casuistry can relieve me of responsibility. Yet even if we would heartily repudiate the approach of Jesuits and other experts in casuistry we may be guilty of choosing our path of conduct on expediency rather than on divinely-given principle.

Chapter 5 opens with an indictment of irresponsible plutocrats who live in style and devote themselves to the pursuit of pleasure whilst oppressing the innocent, helpless poor. The 'Rachmannite' may imagine that he is getting away with it. But he is only storing up retribution for himself (3). Judgement is inevitable and all such injustice—whether ancient or contemporary—cries to high heaven, as we would say (4). Sin still brings its own awful condemnation.

## 88 : False Doctrine

### 2 Peter 2

The second major section of Peter's letter contains his warning against the danger of false teachers and a vehement denunciation of their tactics. He begins by recognizing the fact of their existence and indeed of their inevitability. Jesus Himself had spoken about wolves who would consume the flock (Matt. 7.15–23). As there have been false prophets in the past pretending to have received direct revelations from heaven, so they will be paralleled in the Church by false teachers who distort the truth of the gospel. They will insidiously introduce their own speculations. 'Heresy' stands for self-willed choice, an error which a man insists on asserting in opposition to the apostolic doctrine. In many ways, Peter might have been writing of the twentieth century. We face today an almost unprecedented number of sects, each with its own peculiar doctrines. Some profess a 'higher' truth than that of Scripture, others interpret the Bible in a way that is literally eccentric, i.e. 'off-centre', for the Centre of Scripture is Christ. Such deceivers bring swift destruction on themselves and on those who fall for their perversion of the gospel (1). So serious is any deviation from the truth that it is tantamount to the repudiation of Christ Himself. The Christian way is brought into disrepute (2).

In vs. 4–10 Peter enlarges on the condemnation that awaits such misleading instructions. He picks out three outstanding examples from the past to back up his argument (cf. Gen. 6.1–4; 6.5 ff.; 19.24 f.). These instances are cited (4–6) to show how God does not allow the wicked to escape punishment, but holds them in Hades until the day of judgement (9).

The two sides specially underlined in v. 10a are sexual laxity and disregard for authority, which are in fact the two most obvious expressions of man's sin at the present time. From v. 10b to the end of ch. 2 Peter elaborates on the evil characteristics of the false teachers (cf. Jude 8–13). Irreverence lies at the root of their deviations, for they do not even shrink from reviling 'the glorious ones' (celestial creatures), or the glories of Christ Himself (10b). Many stage, screen and television productions demonstrate man's persistence in this attitude. James saw such men as little better than animals (12). The tragedy is that so many are led astray by their excesses.

Worst of all, such error leads to antinomianism. Unable to distinguish liberty from licence the teachers of whom Peter speaks offered their devotees the wrong kind of free-dom (19), a word constantly misused in contemporary society. In reality such 'freedom' is only the pathway to a deeper bondage. It is a shock to learn that these false teachers had once had an experience of Christ (although some commen-tators understand them to have had only an intellectual appreciation of the gospel). No wonder Peter concludes that it would have been better for them never to have known the way, since they had now forsaken it (21). Such are the depths of sin into which even professing Christians may sink if they apostasize from the truth.

**Questions for further study and discussion on Studies 80–88**

1. Is externalism restricted to the religious non-Christian today or may the true Christian be guilty of it?

2. What are the intellectual roads to salvation without God which are offered in the modern world?

3. Can you understand why the gospel has so often seemed antinomian to some of its critics? What other New Testament passages show clearly that it is not?

4. How far does Rom. 7.7–25 refer to Paul's experience before he became a Christian?

5. To what extent is sin the result of ignorance? Does ignorance excuse sin?

6. In what ways does the expression of sin vary from generation to generation?

7. What are the first questions I should ask of a man on the doorstep who wants to talk to me about religion?

# CHARACTER STUDIES

## 89 : Jeroboam

### 1 Kings 11.26–40; 12.16–33

When Solomon was hard at work building the huge walls and the causeway in the valley between Zion and Moriah, afterwards known as the Valley of the Cheesemongers, an unknown young man distinguished himself by his vigour and gifts of leadership. Solomon noticed him, and advanced him rapidly to rank and influence. He placed him in charge of the levies of labour and monetary contribution from the tribe of Joseph (11.28), that is, of the powerful peoples of Ephraim and Manasseh, for Jeroboam was himself an Ephraimite. Hence this perilous appointment.

Ambition was stirred in the young man's heart, and it was no doubt as he worked among his fellow tribesmen, who, outside of Judah and Benjamin, represented the major strength of Israel, that the able Jeroboam became aware of the deep unrest which seethed beneath the golden surface of Solomon's reign. The old tides of tribal jealousy were beginning to flow in strength. Absalom's rebellion had shown that they were still running. Solomon had done nothing, with his programmes of forced labour and heavy taxation, to check their course. There was pride, too, in the tribes which had once known Joseph's pre-eminence. Joshua, too, had sprung from Ephraim, and his tomb was among his tribesmen at Timnath-serah (Josh. 24.30). Gideon had sprung from them, and Shiloh was in their domain. It was not difficult to stir such feelings to fever-pitch.

It is the art of the demagogue to sense the movement of the crowd and to run ahead. It is easy to cloak a personal ambition in the guise of care for the dignity and welfare of the mass. From ancient times till today, that phenomenon has bedevilled politics. Jeroboam was not a good man, as his subsequent career amply shows, but it was easy in such a day to persuade himself of righteousness. There were undoubted abuses in the land, which united various sections of the community against the régimes. The times called for a leader, and Jeroboam had obvious qualities of leadership. The passion could not be hidden. Shishak of Egypt who, like many others, watched for the end of Solomon's Golden Age, must have heard of Jeroboam, and gave him refuge when Solomon also noted the pernicious strength of his young officer's ambitions. The situation, when Solomon died, was full of menace.

## 90 : Ahijah

### 2 Chronicles 9.29; 1 Kings 11.29–33

In the latter half of Solomon's autocratic reign, the voice of prophecy was silent. Under the shadow of the brilliant king's famous wisdom there were few who were brave enough to speak. Nathan, the old mentor of Solomon's early years, was dead. Then came a notable moment when one man dared to raise his voice. He was chronicler of Solomon's reign, a court scribe recruited from some priestly family of Shiloh, who uttered symbolic prophecy to Jeroboam.

There was bitter abuse in the land. Not only was the kingdom seething with resentment at the heavy burdens laid on men by the vast building projects of the king, and the tensions caused by his apparent favouring of Benjamin and Judah, but Solomon's compromise with paganism was producing its inevitable results. Part of the heritage of the Golden Age was a clutter of paganism (1 Kings 11.33) introduced from the surrounding nations.

The strength of Israel, as Moses and Joshua had warned, was secure only while it was built round the firm centre of their ancient faith. In Solomon's day it was built round the remarkable personality of a clever man. When that central pillar was removed by man's inevitable end, all that had depended upon it fell. The faults and fissures in the nation's structure were plastered over, but by no means closed, and Ahijah saw with clarity the deepest rift of all, when, in his symbolic demonstration of what was to be, he showed the ten northern tribes rent away, and Benjamin and Judah alone remaining true to David's reign. The adherence of Benjamin to the deprived Judah was a

126

geographical accident, due to the fact that the border ran through Jerusalem (Josh. **15**.8; **18**.16; Jer. **20**.2). There was little oneness of mind, for in David's reign we saw a man of Benjamin, one Sheba the son of Bichri, head a revolt against the royal house (2 Sam. **20**.1). So 1 Kings **11**.32 is literally true.

So, with one of those parables of action so dear to the Eastern mind, Jeroboam, on some road through the country-side out of Jerusalem, was made aware that his vast ambitions were to be realized. It is not clear whether divine authority for such a prophecy was granted Ahijah, or whether he assumed it. But it was a brave act, a sincere one, and arose from a sure prescience of events.

# 91 : Rehoboam

## 1 Kings 12.1–5; 2 Chronicles 10

Rehoboam, Solomon's only son, succeeded easily to the throne in 937 B.C. His name ironically means 'enlarger of the people'. David had won and held the northern tribes by the charm of his personality. Solomon had held them by the brilliance with which he had invested the kingdom, and dazzled them by the magnificence of his royalty. It would have required quite extraordinary personal qualities, and a gift for diplomacy of the first order, had the son of an Ammonite woman and a worshipper of Chemosh been able to hold and bind that fragile allegiance.

Significantly the tribes met at Shechem, not Jerusalem. Any perceptive mind would have recognized the storm signals. In this ancient sanctuary, between Mount Ebal and Mount Gerizim, the assembled tribes, as 'men of Israel', determined to bring their very real grievances before the king. Equally significantly, Jeroboam appeared. He had been await-ing the moment.

The offer they made was fair enough. They would accept Rehoboam as king, and maintain the unity of Israel's federa-tion, if he would lighten the burdens that Solomon had laid so oppressively upon them. They wanted only justice, and that was an old instinct of Israel. It is sad to find that a demand so reasonable seems to have taken the young king by surprise. It is obvious that Solomon had done nothing to train his son for leadership, or if he had, he had trained him badly.

Rehoboam took counsel of the old senators and received good advice. To be sure, the words of the old men are not as frank as one might wish them to be. A certain ambiguity, some measure of Solomon's subtlety, infects them, but Rehoboam might have pacified discontent, and gained time for painless change, had he answered them as the old counsellors bade. But 'who knows,' as Solomon asks in Proverbs, 'whether his son will be a wise man or a fool?' A pagan mother and the hothouse atmosphere of the harem were almost a guarantee that he would be a fool.

The court was filled with aristocratic idlers afraid of a diminution in their standards of living. Rehoboam, after long obscurity, was in unaccustomed power. He gave, on the advice of the young men to whom he turned, a fool's answer. Ruin was quite inevitable. Thus David's grandson found his sovereignty shrink to that of a tribe. It was the beginning of endless disaster.

## Questions and themes for further discussion on Studies 89–91

1. Ambition—is it right or wrong?

2. Folly's legacy to posterity.

3. 'He that lacks wisdom asks advice. When advisers conflict, he needs wisdom still more.'